Football Hooliganism in Europe

Also by Anastassia Tsoukala

TERROR, INSECURITY AND LIBERTY

ILLIBERAL PRACTICES OF LIBERAL REGIMES AFTER 9/11 (*co-edited*)

Football Hooliganism in Europe

Security and Civil Liberties in the Balance

Anastassia Tsoukala

Paris XI, France

First published 2009 by
PALGRAVE MACMILLAN

Palgrave Macmillan in the UK is an imprint of Macmillan Publishers Limited, registered in England, company number 785998, of Houndmills, Basingstoke, Hampshire RG21 6XS.

Palgrave Macmillan in the US is a division of St Martin's Press LLC, 175 Fifth Avenue, New York, NY 10010.

Palgrave Macmillan is the global academic imprint of the above companies and has companies and representatives throughout the world.

Palgrave® and Macmillan® are registered trademarks in the United States, the United Kingdom, Europe and other countries.

ISBN-13: 978–0–230–20114–9 hardback
ISBN-10: 0–230–20114–8 hardback

This book is printed on paper suitable for recycling and made from fully managed and sustained forest sources. Logging, pulping and manufacturing processes are expected to conform to the environmental regulations of the country of origin.

A catalogue record for this book is available from the British Library.

Library of Congress Cataloging-in-Publication Data
Tsoukala, Anastassia.
    Football hooliganism in Europe : security and civil liberties in the balance / Anastassia Tsoukala.
        p. cm.
    Includes bibliographical references and index.
    ISBN 978–0–230–20114–9
    1. Soccer hooliganism—Europe.   2. Soccer—Social aspects.
    3. Spectator control.   4. Civil rights—Europe.   I. Title.
    GV943.9.F35T76 2009
    796.334—dc22   2008043237

10   9   8   7   6   5   4   3   2   1
18   17   16   15   14   13   12   11   10   09

Printed and bound in Great Britain by
CPI Antony Rowe, Chippenham and Eastbourne

For Ilias

Contents

Acknowledgements

This book is the product of twenty years' research into football hooliganism in Europe. However, several of the ideas underlying parts of it had their origins, and were further developed, in the context of various research projects: the analysis of the tension between security and liberty first featured in CHALLENGE – *The Changing Landscape of European Liberty and Security*, a research project funded by the Sixth Framework Programme of the European Commission's Directorate-General for Research (2004–9); the study of the evolution of domestic and EU counter-hooliganism policing policies formed part of a research project on the combating of football hooliganism in France, funded by INHES/French Interior Ministry (2005–7); the analysis of the social construction of threat emerged from COST Action A24, *The Evolving Social Construction of Threats*, a research project funded by the European Scientific Fund (2004–7).

This work has also been shaped by countless thought-provoking conversations with Didier Bigo, with whom I have the happy privilege of sharing not only a substantial part of my professional life but also many carefree moments of friendship. I would furthermore like to express my deep gratitude to an old friend Spyros Georgantas, for all his invaluable assistance in developing my own library and, by extension, my academic skills.

Needless to say, this work would have never been possible without the input of many police and intelligence officials who, over the years, have been willing to impart at least some of their knowledge to me, for which I warmly thank them.

Last but not least, I am most grateful to Marion Marshrons for not only helping me to get to grips with the finer points of the English language but also for her careful and patient editing.

No man is an island, entire of itself; every man is a piece of the continent, a part of the main. If a clod be washed away by the sea, Europe is the less, as well as if a promontory were, as well as if a manor of thy friend's or of thine own were. Any man's death diminishes me, because I am involved in mankind; and therefore never send to know for whom the bell tolls; it tolls for thee.

John Donne, *Devotions upon Emergent Occasions,*
Meditation XVII (1623)

Introduction

Crowd disorder at sporting events is nothing new. Football-related violence more specifically was often a feature of nineteenth-century fixtures in the UK (Dunning et al. 1988; Frosdick and Marsh 2005) and, by the beginning of the twentieth century, had become commonplace in many European football stadia. The phenomenon has, however, undergone a series of significant changes, which began among British football crowds during the 1960s. Violent incidents gradually ceased to emanate from ordinary sports crowds and instead stemmed from the actions of ever-younger perpetrators, usually adolescents and post-adolescents, for whom such behaviour had a whole range of meanings, rooted in real or imaginary worlds, that were necessary for the shaping of their personalities, be they individual, social or political. At the same time, violent incidents went from being spontaneous, emotionally linked to the progress of matches and located in a space–time dimension that was well defined by the sporting venue and the length of the fixture to being increasingly organized, disengaged from match-related emotions and located in an undefined space–time dimension, randomly including urban and peri-urban areas and the periods before and after matches.

From the 1970s onwards, this type of collective violence, commonly known as football hooliganism, spread rapidly across several European countries, resulting in the establishment, first at the national level and, from 1985 onwards, also at the European Community and European levels,[1] of numerous control measures which have become increasingly repressive. As the implementation of such counter-hooliganism policies created a complex web of interactions between social control agents and the young football supporters targeted, from then on the development of the phenomenon and the forms in which it manifested itself reflected reactive mutual dependency rather than autonomous action, with the strategies and methods of action employed by the troublemakers gradually turning into 'survival reactions' for dealing with the constraints imposed on them by the social control apparatus. In this ever-growing arena of interaction, involving national and supranational legislators, public and private security agencies, intelligence officers, judges, local politicians, sports officials, social educators, members of extremist political organizations, journalists, academics and football supporters' clubs, football hooliganism and its control inevitably became focal points for a whole range of often conflicting political, social, economic and cultural stakes. The phenomenon continued to evolve under the combined effect of these influences, becoming more radical,[2] encompassing other sports[3] and new areas, gradually moving out of first division stadia and into other urban areas and/or lower division stadia, and, in its current form – namely fights organized outside any sporting context at meeting places agreed in advance between football hooligans – becoming to a certain degree autonomous of sporting events *stricto sensu*.

Defining football hooliganism

While this constant transformation of the phenomenon demonstrates its resilience, it also raises questions about our ability to grasp its essence. First of all, it should be pointed out that the factors that determined the emergence of football hooliganism are not necessarily the same as those that have influenced its subsequent development, which has been marked by the interventions of a whole host of public and private actors, with each stage of that development moreover adhering to its own particular structuring patterns. So, apart from accepting that they both entail opposition to an adversary that is initially or permanently perceived in the context of a sporting event, what do the football hooliganism of the 1960s and that of today have in common? Second, the motives of the actors can be so deeply rooted in national specificities that they make any comparative approach particularly difficult. While football-related incidents may appear to share many features, their causes may differ greatly according to the context in which they occur. For example, they may be connected with conflicts over identity, politics or religion; the perpetrators may come from different socio-economic or cultural backgrounds, and so on. Consequently, setting aside any similarities there may be in terms of the way they manifest themselves, and given the deep differences at the causal level, is it possible to say that they have anything in common? If football hooliganism is a generic term that refers to an array of actions with a variety of meanings, depending on the period and the country of origin of the actors, would it be unrealistic to endeavour to define it?

The challenge of attempting to set in stone a firm definition of a social reality that is highly fluid has certainly spurred scholars to action. For over forty years, they have looked into the issue and produced more and more studies covering many academic disciplines. Nevertheless, they have failed to construct any explanatory frames that might be acceptable to all or most academics. Such studies, which were first developed in the UK in the early 1970s, increased in number in the second half of the 1980s, following the Heysel tragedy.[4] In fact, that dramatic event had a twofold influence on the development of the study of football hooliganism in Europe because, on the one hand, it speeded up further British studies and, on the other, acted as a spur for the vast majority of studies conducted in other European countries, such as France, Italy, Germany, Belgium, the Netherlands, Greece and Spain. However, though quantitatively significant, this influence was short-lived since the number of research studies into the causes of the phenomenon declined continuously throughout the 1990s and, by the beginning of the twenty-first century, had stagnated at a very low level. Paradoxically, this reduction in the number of works on the aetiology of the issue, which stemmed from the fact that the academic community had run out of steam and that the public authorities were reluctant to carry on funding research into a phenomenon which they claimed by then to be managing satisfactorily, has nevertheless had a positive effect in that it has made it easier to stand back and cast a critical eye over them.

In fact, although these explanatory theories shed light on several aspects of football hooliganism, they suffer from many shortcomings. The first is their failure to be multidisciplinary. Each addresses the issue from a single viewpoint, which means that, however relevant it may be, it ends up simplifying the multiple facets of the origin and subsequent development of the phenomenon. This disciplinary compartmentalization is coupled with spatial compartmentalization. Comparative approaches are extremely rare and edited volumes dealing with case studies from more than one country have failed to grasp all the subtleties of the cases in question or to highlight any possible compelling trends in the manifestation and/or control of the issue in Europe. Besides, in none of these studies has a distinction been made between the factors that may have contributed to the emergence of football hooliganism and those which entered the equation later as a result of its specific dynamics and the web of interactions developed between it and many institutions and social groups.

Furthermore, the subject matter they cover is extremely diverse, making it particularly difficult to classify them. It is telling in this regard that the only book which has so far attempted to set out the main explanatory theories concerning football hooliganism in Europe (Frosdick and Marsh 2005) failed to distinguish them according to any kind of scientific criterion but was confined to presenting them by the nationality or the name of the scholars, their proximity to a school of thought or their adherence to certain epistemological trends. In addition, despite being the fullest of all the overviews in quantitative terms, it remains qualitatively weak since, precisely because of the absence of a valid classification criterion, it fails to establish the analogies that need to be made between the British theories and those of other European researchers. Other scholars have certainly tried to present these theories in a critical fashion by employing a range of different classification criteria, but they have been unable to produce any generally applicable classification tools because, on the one hand, they have confined their comments mainly to British research (Taylor 1982b: 165–80; Hobbs and Robins 1991; Giulianotti 1994; Dunning et al. 2002: 13–15) and, on the other, their criticisms have rarely extended beyond polemic to become scientific analysis in the true sense of the term. It is worth stressing here that the adoption of a highly polemical stance on the part of the upholders of various theories, which has predominated within British academia since the early 1990s,[5] has been damaging to the overall work on the subject because, by focusing researchers' attention on certain aspects of the aetiology of football hooliganism, it has ended up by removing from international debate virtually any consideration of the social control of the phenomenon and the interplay between the actions of football hooligans and the decisions and practices of the actors involved in dealing with the issue.

This weakening of the academic community's role as definer of a social phenomenon is all the more serious in that, combined with the fact that there is no legal definition of football hooliganism, it has left the power to define it in the hands of social control agents. Continuously engaged in that definitional struggle, the latter have developed their own perceptions, mainly centred on the notion of the dangerousness of football hooligans, and disseminated them within the public arena. In the absence of a strong platform from which to broadcast any counter-arguments, those perceptions have ended up becoming the accepted frameworks for understanding reality. Yet, as has often been emphasized since the 1960s, defining complex social issues entails much more than a simple conceptual delimiting of the so-called objective elements of the matter to be defined; it is also a highly political enterprise since the subjectivity implicit in selecting the elements that go to make up a definition, as well as in understanding them and correlating them with the surrounding world, cannot be dissociated from the social or political positions held by the authors of such definitions (Becker 1963; Erikson 1966; Cohen 1972; Spector and Kitsuse 1977; Hall et al. 1978; Edelman 1988; Goode and Ben-Yehuda 1994; Thompson 1998). Though purporting to establish generally accurate explanatory frames, public discourses, especially when addressing behaviour seen as threatening to internal security, in fact reflect ideological schemes, political and social interests and interpretation frameworks that have been influenced by the issues and values prioritized by the institutions or social groups to which the definers belong. Being political in nature, this advocacy of certain frameworks for interpreting reality at the expense of others generates many political effects. As part of a logic of government, in the Foucauldian sense, it helps to determine the potential fields of action of others (Foucault 1984), not only by consolidating the position of the definers both within the field to which they belong and other related fields but also, and above all, by providing a solid basis for the legitimization of any relevant control measures. Starting from the premise that 'there is no power relation without the correlative constitution of a field of knowledge, nor any knowledge that does not presuppose or constitute at the same time power relations' (Foucault 1975: 32), the construction and dissemination of knowledge are indissociable from the operations of power (Lacombe 1993). Thus, the authority conferred on those who possess knowledge of football hooliganism legitimizes them in their struggle for power, be it material or non-material, vis-à-vis other actors who are directly or indirectly involved in dealing with the issue, and further legitimizes, in the eyes of civil society, the establishment of control apparatuses which, in this instance, have become increasingly detrimental to the fundamental freedoms of those against whom they are targeted. While power–knowledge relations can be constantly reinforced by the mutual legitimization that goes on between all the actors involved in these processes, in the specific case of social control agents they can also be perpetuated by means of circular logic, with knowledge being translated into control practices which generate new knowledge, which prompts redefinition of the phenomenon to be controlled, leading to the adoption of new control mechanisms, and so on. The effects of domination thus produced, which are often seen at the regulatory level, include mainly 'dispositions, manœuvres, tactics, techniques, [and] functionings' (Foucault 1975: 31), that is, anything that comprises the everyday management of football hooliganism by social control agents.

This mutual dependency between the processes by which football hooliganism is defined and those which control it, on which this book will seek to shed as much light as possible, is all the more important because it can also provide an understanding of the conditions that have given rise to the enormous indifference exhibited so far by civil society across Europe in the face of numerous attacks on the civil liberties of people accused or suspected of being involved in football hooliganism. Standing in sharp contrast to the increasing dynamism found within human rights circles and the constant mobilization of many different kinds of support for the rights of a wide range of social groups, society's long silence on the curbing of the rights of such people is puzzling. Subjected to a process of constant stigmatization which has been accompanied, as this book will seek to show, by a splintered definitional process that mirrors the evolving (inter)national security stakes, have football hooligans been turned into such dangerous social enemies that they no longer deserve our attention when their rights are transgressed?

Controlling football hooliganism

Over the past few decades, many studies from different epistemological fields have drawn attention to the increasingly important position that security has occupied on the European political agenda, especially since the end of the Cold War. Political scientists and criminologists, in particular those representing critical tendencies within their respective branches, have thus examined the growing politicization of security issues (Waever et al. 1993; Bigo 1994, 2002, 2008; Lipshutz 1995; Huysmans 1995, 2004, 2006; Anderson 1996; Buzan et al. 1998; Ceyhan and Tsoukala 2002; Nikolopoulos 2002; Ericson 2007), the gradual blurring of the conceptual and operational boundaries between external and internal security (Bigo 1999, 2000, 2001), the emergence of security providers from outside the public sphere (Bayley and Shearing 1996; Ericson and Haggerty 1997; Loader 2000; Johnston and Shearing 2003; Dorn and Levi 2007; Loader and Walker 2007), the transnationalization of policing (Bigo 1992, 1996; Sheptycki 2000, 2002) and the rapid spread throughout the political class and the security world of a new perception of threat that relies on both conceptual unification (Bigo 1994) and depoliticization. In their attempts to study states' reactions to security threats and the role of security and media professionals in the (re)construction of public problem arenas, these researchers have sought to analyse the reconfiguration of the political and security fields, reveal the securitization processes at work and show how the emergence of postmodern societies faced with new risks, and therefore required to find new strategies for dealing with them (Beck 1992; Castel 2003; Bauman 2007), has, among other things, profoundly influenced the design and implementation of crime control policies.

Issues such as the increasing focus given to actuarial risk management principles by these crime control policies and the impact that such a proactive pattern of action has on the relationship of crime and the criminal with time, space, the victim and even reality, as well as on the goals of the action taken by the social control apparatus, have already been widely studied and remain central to criminological debate, both in Europe and across the Atlantic (Garland 1985; Feeley and Simon 1992; Simon 1997; Ericson and Haggerty 1997; De Giorgi 2000; Shearing 2001; Mary and Papatheodorou 2001; Silver and Miller 2002; Feeley 2003; Johnston and Shearing 2003; Hörnqvist 2004; Papatheodorou and Mary 2006). Prompted by these same changes in the crime control realm, as well as by the emergence of new technologies of control, other sociologists, political scientists and criminologists have focused on the power-related interests and strategies underlying the spread of new remote-monitoring devices, as well as on the concomitant transformation of the relationship between technology, society and the individual (Lyon 1994, 2001, 2004; Jones 2000; Graham and Wood 2003; Bonditti 2004; Bigo 2004; Froment and Kaluszynski 2006; Ceyhan 2007).

Since the early 1990s, many analyses of the changes that have taken place in the security realm have focused on the criminalization processes of certain social groups associated with various 'public problems', such as illegal immigration, juvenile delinquency and urban violence (Mils and Thrännhardt 1995; Palidda 1997; Marshall 1997; Dal Lago 1999; Wacquant 1999b; Mucchielli 2001; Tsoukala 2002, 2005; Bonelli 2003, 2007, 2008; Lagrange 2003; Mucchielli et al. 2006). The terrorist attacks of 11 September 2001, far from diminishing this interest in the constantly changing relationship between social control and civil society, have tended to consolidate these key research questions by putting the tension between freedom and security at the heart of the debate, following the introduction in almost every country of Europe of legal frameworks which, in the name of effectively fighting terrorism, infringe civil liberties. Many legal, sociological and criminological studies have thus denounced the attacks that have taken place on the principles of the rule of law (Waldron 2003; Leone and Anrig 2003; Haubrich 2003; Brouwer et al. 2003; Scheppele 2004; Balzacq and Carrera 2006; Baldaccini and Guild 2006; Starmer 2007) and revealed how the arguments justifying the adoption of liberticidal laws were constructed (Johnson 2002; Steinert 2003; Tsoukala 2004a, 2006a, 2006c, 2008a, 2009; Lazar and Lazar 2004; Leudar et al. 2004; Altheide 2006; Hodges and Nilep 2007), giving rise to the fear of the eventual establishment of a more permanent change in the relationship between citizens and the executive. Given the possibility that a permanent state of emergency, or at least one conceived as such, could well be introduced, other studies have questioned Giorgio Agamben's theories on exceptionalism (1997, 2002) by analysing the nature of states of emergency and the relationship between the rule of law and politics in a democracy (Guild 2003a, 2003b; Bigo 2007).

However, this plethora of studies on the changes that have taken place in the security realm and their impact on the configuration of the fields of politics and security, on the one hand, and the relationship between politics and civil society, on the other, has rarely included football hooliganism. Somewhat paradoxically, very few scholars have sought to examine the policing of football hooliganism in Europe. For the most part, the issue has been presented briefly, in a few pages (Giulianotti 1994; Della Porta 1998; Basson 2004; Waddington 2007), described in detail but uncritically (Chatard 1994; Bodin and Trouilhet 2002; T.M.C. Asser Instituut 2004), or addressed empirically rather than theoretically (Comeron 1992, 2002; Comeron and Vanbellingen 2002). On the rare occasion when studies have looked at it in depth, they have been limited in scope because they have been confined to examining the behaviour of English football supporters abroad (Garland and Rowe 2000) or focused on a single aspect of the social control of the phenomenon by analysing, for example, the control of racism in stadia (Garland and Rowe 1999b) or the arbitrary nature of certain police practices (Trivizas 1980, 1984; Williams 1980; Armstrong 1994; Armstrong and Hobbs 1994; Armstrong and Young 1997; Marchi 2005). In those cases where the issue has been addressed comprehensively (Lewis 1980; Mignon 1993, 1996, 1998; De Biasi 1996), the analyses carried out have struggled to be anything other than descriptive and have generally made no attempt to relate it to the strategies and interests that underlie the design and establishment of security policies at the national, EU and international levels.

Despite their heuristic interest, some in-depth studies tend to be limited in time and space, and/or their scope. Thus, while the research undertaken by Rocco de Biasi (1998), Gary Armstrong, both alone (1998) and in collaboration with Clive Norris and Jade Moran (Norris et al. 1998), and, more recently, by Megan O'Neill (2004, 2006) offers valuable insights into the methods and practices used to police football hooliganism, and provides us with excellent analyses of the way law enforcers perceive and address the issue, it remains nothing more than a series of national or even local monographs. Consequently, it does not enable us to grasp the existing transnational policing schemes or to discern the interplay between the adoption of such schemes and general developments within the security field. The pioneering works of Otto Adang (Adang and Cuvelier 2001) and Clifford Stott (Stott and Reicher 1998; Stott 2003; Stott et al. 2006, 2007) clearly show the importance of the interactions that take place in the course of face-to-face contacts between security officials and football supporters, and demonstrate, for the first time, the links that exist between the behaviour of the latter and the crowd management strategies implemented in a given context. However, the conclusions they draw from their extensive field research have not been correlated with the current configuration of the political and security fields within which the security officials under examination are operating. Largely depoliticized and put forward with a view to promoting models of good policing practice, they do not allow us to understand the conceptual frames and interests that underlie the way those officials perceive the issue or the processes that determine the shaping of the counter-hooliganism policies that officials on the ground are obliged to implement.

The least studied of all aspects of counter-hooliganism policies is still the question of regulation. At the national level, apart from some in-depth analyses (Lamberti 1988; Pearson 1999, 2005; Stott and Pearson 2006; Mark and Pearson 2006; Cortesi 2007), the normative framework used to control football hooliganism has so far only had a few pages devoted to it, often in the context of books on more general topics (Greenfield and Osborn 1998, 2001: 22–38; Simon 2008). In comparative law, with the exception of my own analysis of the regulation of football hooliganism in England and Italy (Tsoukala 1995), there is only one study comparing the situations in England and Australia (Warren 2003). Lastly, at the European level, apart from two legal analyses of the 1985 European Convention (Sims and Tsitsoura 1987; Taylor 1987) and my own study of the measures taken by UEFA, the Council of Europe and European Community bodies (Tsoukala 1995: 201–28), there are just a few uncommented overviews, covering either the key legal provisions and police measures introduced by each EU Member State to deal with the phenomenon (T.M.C. Asser Instituut 2004), or the EU's involvement in the fight against hooliganism (Miège 2002; Mojet 2005).

In this first attempt at unravelling the strategies and political, social and security stakes underlying the development of counter-hooliganism policies in Europe, which has largely taken its inspiration from the above-mentioned works on the evolution of security-related issues in Europe, I seek to analyse the interactions between the security field as a whole and the counter-hooliganism policies established at the European, EU, national and, where applicable, local levels. These inter- actions, which have developed over the past four decades, reflect the general changes that have occurred in the fields of politics and security in Europe during that period and the impact such changes have had on counter-hooliganism policies.

This study does not pretend to be an exhaustive analysis of all aspects of domestic counter-hooliganism policies. Nor does it seek to shed light on the way football hooliganism is actually policed at the national level. By highlighting certain facets of the web of interactions underlying how the issue is defined and controlled, it attempts to provide a better understanding of the strategies and methods used to regulate and police football hooliganism in Europe. At the same time, in so doing, it allows us to grasp a reality that stands in stark contrast to the current debate on the breaches of civil liberties being committed in European countries in the name of protecting internal security. Indeed, while reflection on the current tension between freedom and security derives mainly from analysing the security policies set in place after 11 September 2001, the present study of counter-hooliganism policies reveals the slow but sure establishment of a control of deviance with regard to football support- ers, the increasing expansion of which relies implicitly on broad social consensus. Rather than limiting itself to examining the recent introduc- tion, under current counter-terrorism policies, of supposedly temporary emergency measures and seeing the jeopardizing of the rule of law as simply a transient political episode, it describes how the breaches of civil liberties that have taken place in the context of the day-to-day polic- ing of football hooliganism have gradually become institutionalized. There is nothing special about such breaches. They reflect the profound changes that have taken place in the security field since the end of the Cold War and are inherent to the structure and operational logic of the prevailing social control model which has shaped the regulatory frame- work and policing of football hooliganism since 1985. Thus, forming part of a continuum rather than being a break with the past, they signal a gradual erosion of civil liberties which, quite simply, has spread and gathered pace since the terrorist attacks that took place at the beginning of the twenty-first century.

Methodology

Though concentrating on football hooliganism, this book is the product of twenty years' research into not only that subject but also immigration and terrorism, all undertaken in the context of individual or collective national and EU research programmes. It relies on relevant research and reflection from the fields of law, criminology, the sociology of deviance, and of policing and social control, political sociology and international relations. As well as taking advantage of numerous secondary sources, it makes use of more than 70 interviews with security professionals in six European countries[6] and many analyses of public discourses at the EU and national levels.[7]

The geographical scope of the study is much more varied than the book title would suggest. As far as analysis of academic theories, the normative framework and the policing of the issue are concerned, all European countries which, on the one hand, have been affected by football hooliganism since the 1970s and, on the other, have been liberal democracies for most of the period in question are covered. The consequence of this is that the countries of Western Europe which, for a variety of reasons we cannot go into here, have been relatively untouched by the phenomenon[8] and the countries of Central and Eastern Europe which, though affected by football hooliganism (Brimson 2003; Smolik 2004; Beiu 2005), were for many years under Communist rule, are omitted. The regulation and policing of football hooliganism is further examined at both the European and EU levels. On the other hand, the public discourses analysed here are taken from the French and British press, from 1970 to the present day, the Italian press, from 1970 to 1985 and from 1995 onwards, the Greek press since 1985 and the Belgian press since 2000. At the EU level, public discourses from all relevant European Parliament debates since the mid-1990s have been examined.

The issues addressed are presented chronologically. Although it is not always easy to draw clear dividing lines that closely match all the national specificities of the different European countries, I believe that, by using the degree of clarity of legislative and law enforcement responses to the phenomenon as a yardstick, the policy frameworks employed during the period under examination can be divided into three stages which can be described as clear (1965–85), blurred

(1985–97) and splintered (1997–2008). Within each stage I look at the four main topics on which the definition and control of football hooliganism hinge: academic definitions, the normative framework, policing and public discourses. In the case of the academic definitions, which come from over ninety researchers in twelve European countries, I have presented them according to the discipline to which they belong.[9]

Part I
Clear Contours (1965–85)

Introduction to Part I

The changes that took place in the behaviour of football supporters from the mid-1960s onwards rapidly attracted the attention of the academic community. However, although this type of collective violence quickly spread to several countries of mainland Europe,[1] only British researchers were looking into its aetiology during this period. Their theories, which took their inspiration from many psychological, anthropological and sociological schools of thought, mainly sought to explain the phenomenon by analysing the behaviour of football supporters and, in some cases, the role of the media. Although these initial explanatory frames were later often criticized, their influence, both within the UK and abroad, was long-lived.

Despite the growth of football hooliganism in Europe and the increasing seriousness of violent incidents at national and international matches,[2] in terms of its social control the phenomenon was still seen as an ordinary public order problem. Consequently, apart from UEFA's security guidelines, there was no supranational regulation. At the national level, its control relied on general normative frameworks and ordinary police strategies that had been shaped by the national specificities of each of the countries concerned.

National specificities were also at the root of the significant disparities in domestic public discourses which, in fact, reflected the socio-political context from which they emerged. Thus, while in the UK, for example, public discourses started to place ever greater emphasis on the danger posed by football hooligans, thereby triggering the first moral panic over the issue, elsewhere, in Italy for example, a more moderate and even lenient line was taken towards this type of youth violence.

1
Early Academic Theories

1 Psychological theses

Developed between the mid-1970s and the early 1980s, the first psychological theses made use of the ethogenic paradigm which they borrowed from social psychology. They are best set out in the work of the team led by Peter Marsh (Marsh et al. 1978; Marsh 1978; Marsh and Campbell 1982), which emphasized the symbolic nature of football hooliganism, seeing it as ritualized rather than actual violence. Such behaviour was thus a ritual display of violence, labelled by Marsh as *aggro*,[1] which allowed young football supporters to assert their virility by impressing their adversaries and demonstrating their membership of micro-cultures. Consequently, any crossing over from this ritual display to real violence would be accidental and infrequent, arising either because a minority of young football supporters within a particular group had failed to comply with its tacit rules or because the law enforcement agencies had intervened inappropriately.

This thesis also underlined the existence of a genuine order on stadium terraces which, behind their apparent disorder, were places where social identity was constructed. It argued that, far from acting chaotically, young football supporters, searching for a symbolic balance between group loyalty and their desire to be aggressive, embarked on an actual three-stage 'career'[2] which, through peer recognition, could give them the reputation and status denied them by the rest of society. Openly carrying on from the work of Goffman on the construction of moral careers as a means of boosting personal reputation (Goffman 1968, 1973), Marsh did not explicitly rule out the influence of the interactionist current, but made it clear that he saw the career of a football supporter as being a process that was much less mechanical than other types of delinquent careers described by some American criminologists (Becker 1963; Wolfgang et al. 1972).

These works, which shed light on the role played by context in defining the meaning football supporters attribute to their violent behaviour, had merit in that, using field research, they were the first to put forward a rational interpretation of football hooliganism by debunking preconceived ideas about the irrationality of the phenomenon. Although some scholars later considered the repertory of tacit rules drawn up by Marsh and his team to be incomplete (Roversi and Balestri 2000: 188–9), the strength of this thesis lay in its uncovering of what, from then on, became known as the 'social order of the terraces'.

This theory nevertheless remains open to criticism because, on the one hand, it underestimates the extent of the actual violence and, on the other, the phenomenon is completely dissociated from its historical context. In the case of the former, it should be noted that incidents of real violence were much more frequent than Marsh's team led us to understand, thereby calling into question their supposed accidental nature. Furthermore, the ritual violence thesis did not cater for the subsequent development of football hooliganism since it failed to explain the appearance of forms of violence which, given their nature, precluded any notion of ritual. Certain acts which, *a priori*, did not involve physical contact, such as the throwing of missiles, were thus left unexplained.

As far as the second criticism of the ritual violence thesis is concerned, the picture of football hooliganism it gave was not contextualized because no consideration was given to either the socio-economic and political profile of the actors or to the specificities of their social milieu. The thesis therefore remains loosely formulated, completely detached from any kind of space–time framework and, as a consequence, incapable of revealing the nature of football hooligans as social actors and the socio-economic and political factors that might be linked to the appearance of this type of collective violence.

2 Anthropological theses

The anthropological theories are, in some respects, similar to the psychological ones to the extent that they too focus on the meaning accorded to football hooliganism by young supporters, while stressing the highly ritualized and symbolic nature of their behaviour. Thus, in the early 1980s, Desmond Morris saw the football match as a major social event built on a system of symbols mainly centred on hunting, war, religious practice and collective representation (Morris 1981). According to this thesis, which was later taken up by many others (e.g. Augé 1982; Brohm 1983, 1993; Onofri and Ricci 1984; Bromberger et al. 1987; Ehrenberg et al. 1987; Dal Lago 1990a, 1990b; Bromberger 1998; Vassort 1999: 275–348; De Biasi 2002; Zahopoulos 2004), this powerful symbolic world quite naturally invited all those involved in it to adopt symbolic behaviour, manifested in the performance of ritualized acts. Football hooliganism was thus part of a set of football-related rites involving club officials and players, as well as supporters. The latter, in particular, established actual tribes with their own dress code, emblems and modes of communication and behaviour. Within this tribal milieu, the place accorded to violence was certainly important, but its purpose remained essentially symbolic. It was therefore rare for it to devolve into real violence, with most incidents consisting of threats rather than physical violence.

Despite being of undeniable interest in that they demonstrated the complexity of the violent behaviour of football supporters, these theses attract the same criticisms as the psychological theories to the extent that they focus on the ritual and symbolic aspects of football hooliganism and underestimate the extent and seriousness of the actual violence. Furthermore, and something for which they have often been criticized (Redhead 1991: 481; Dunning et al. 1991), their findings are based on such limited fields of enquiry that they cannot possibly give rise to any broader conclusions without running the risk of being seen as mere extrapolations.

3 Sociological theses

The sociological theses developed during this period borrow from various currents of thought, including political sociology, subcultural theories and the sociology of deviance.

3.1 Theories founded on political sociology

At the end of the 1960s, Ian Taylor, taking his inspiration from Marxism, sought to establish links between football hooliganism and the way the British working class operated. According to his thesis, football supporters' clubs formed part of a football subculture founded on a kind of participatory democracy involving the spectators on the one hand, and the players and club officials on the other. However, once football became professionalized, internationalized and subject to the law of the market, such democracy gradually disappeared. This provoked a reaction on the part of the supporters who, hostile to the process of embourgeoisement of the game, refused to go from playing an active role as supporters to a passive one as spectators/consumers and responded violently to this social distancing and the weakening of their relations with their clubs. So, football hooliganism could be seen as a resistance movement organized by the working class, who felt they were being deprived of their favourite leisure activity (Taylor 1969, 1971a, 1971b; Taylor and Wall 1976). Taken up again by John Clarke and Tony Jefferson (1976: 141–2), as we shall see later, Taylor's work was influential for a long time both inside the country and abroad, but it also drew much criticism.

In certain respects, his thesis is still relevant today to the extent that it provides one of the earliest analyses of the changes that took place in football from the 1960s onwards and their impact on football supporters. However, it does not succeed in putting forward a satisfactory theory of the phenomenon it wishes to explain because it relies on a romantic view of the past, whereas the existence of a united working class seeing football clubs as participatory democracies has never actually been shown, least of all in England (Dunning et al. 1988: 30–1).[3] In his later work, Taylor accepted these criticisms and he put forward an alternative theory in which he argued that football hooliganism was a symptom of the decomposition of a specifically working-class spectator sport. Consequently, it reflected the alienation of the working class itself which, caught in a trap brought about by the repeated transformation and fragmentation of an increasingly liberal labour market, was no longer able to hand on to its young people its traditional socialization systems. Given the psychological and material frustrations underlying this process of alienation, violence seemed to be the only appropriate response (Taylor 1982a, 1982b, 1986).

Yet, even in its revised form, Taylor's thesis remains very limited because it relies solely on the social origin of English football hooligans. Linking the emergence and development of football hooliganism to the evolution of the British working class in the postwar period does not explain the presence and scale of the phenomenon in Scotland, for example, or in other European countries, such as Italy, Germany, the Netherlands, France, Greece and Cyprus, where hooligans are not predominantly of working-class origin and where, in any event, the working class has not evolved in the same way as it has done in England.

3.2   Subcultural theses

Developed in the 1950s in the United States, the concept of a delinquent subculture has enjoyed great popularity among criminologists (Cohen

1955; Cloward and Ohlin 1960; Szabo 1966; Wolfgang and Ferracuti 1967; Cusson 1981). According to the latter, juvenile delinquency could be ascribed to the existence of a delinquent subculture among young people from disadvantaged social classes who, denied access to the middle classes, create a value system that is coherent, but at odds with the dominant social and moral norms and end up adopting delinquent and even violent behaviour. This concept, which spread rapidly through the social sciences, appealed to certain researchers working on football hooliganism who saw it as one of the main explanations for the phenomenon. Thus, through his study of skinheads as precursors of football hooligans, John Clarke (1976) took both the social origin and youth of the latter into consideration and concluded that football hooliganism was a symbolic social interaction emanating from an age group that had formed its own subculture in order to assert its identity in the face of parental authority on the one hand, and the rest of society on the other. From this point of view, young football supporters were just one example of the rapid emergence of youth as a new social actor in search of emancipation and self-affirmation within the emerging consumer society. Young football supporters, frequently born into a working class that had been gradually dispossessed of its favourite leisure activity and caught up in a dialectic between a hegemonic dominant culture and a subordinate parental one, sought to develop their own value system by encouraging negative behaviour models as a reaction against a dominant culture that prized the attainment of long-term goals, taking personal responsibility and a whole range of codified standards on how to behave in public above instant gratification (Clarke et al. 1976). Once these negative behaviour models became part of the process whereby football was turned into a commercial leisure activity, they started to imitate aspects of the game itself so that violence on the terraces became an extension of the sporting contest (Clarke 1978).

By thus linking football-related violence to the changes taking place in British society as a whole and in popular leisure pursuits in particular, Clarke's work clearly contradicted the then dominant thesis, still regularly repeated today, which argued that football hooligans were not 'genuine' supporters. Furthermore, as noted by Steve Frosdick and Peter Marsh (2005: 91–2), his work complemented and reinforced Taylor's by giving it the empirical aspect it was lacking. However, the thesis of an age-related subculture, emerging against a background of working-class alienation, cannot satisfactorily explain football hooliganism because, as we have seen, it does not apply in countries where football hooligans do not come mainly from the working class.

3.3   Theses founded on the sociology of deviance

In the 1970s, many researchers, influenced by the emerging interactionist school and the works of its representatives on the socio-cultural factors and processes affecting deviant behaviour and the underlying social construction of reality (Becker 1963; Lemert 1967), sought to attribute football hooliganism to a media-induced process of deviancy amplification. The first advocate of this thesis, Stanley Cohen, thus saw football hooliganism as the product of a moral panic that had been created and fuelled by the media. Following on from his work on the social construction of deviance (Cohen 1972), Cohen analysed how the media emphasized the seriousness of the threat posed by football hooligans by systematically using various methods of discursively constructing social enemies in general which relied mainly on exaggeration and distortion, thereby helping to ensure that middle- and upper-class fears about anything that might threaten the status quo became embodied in football hooligans (Cohen 1973). Reinforced some years later by the Marxist-inspired work of Stuart Hall and his team on the social and political issues underlying the appearance of 'social problems' and the implementation of public policies for dealing with them (Hall et al. 1978), this thesis found considerable favour in academic circles and gave rise to several pieces of research which, while still not seeing it as a cause of football hooliganism, clearly demonstrated the bias that existed in media coverage of the phenomenon (Hall 1978; Whannel 1979).

These days, it is widely accepted that, in order to understand the current scale of football hooliganism, it is essential to take into consideration the role played by the media in amplifying deviance. Nevertheless, primary responsibility for the emergence and development of football hooliganism cannot be laid at the door of the mass media because this would be to dissociate the phenomenon from its historical context and, with the human factor also being disregarded, to reduce it to a simple, quasi-mechanical social process. To this should be added the reservations some researchers have expressed about the true impact the media have had on the growth of football hooliganism. Quite apart from the fact that any assessment of the media's impact on the formation of public opinion in general still poses insurmountable methodological difficulties (Jewkes 2004; Maigret 2004), its influence on the growth of football hooliganism in particular should be put in perspective by bearing in mind that, throughout the 1970s, the UK media consistently under- rather than overestimated the scale of the phenomenon since pre- and post-match incidents were rarely reported (Taylor 1982a: 71–3).

The same applied from the end of the 1980s onwards when they began to minimize or even ignore many incidents taking place at matches in the lower divisions in order to support the argument that football hooliganism had been eradicated from English stadia (Redhead 1997: 24–5; Dunning 1999: 133; Dunning 2000: 147–50) and therefore expedite the return of English clubs to European competition.[4] Yet, though it would be advisable at this point to bear in mind one of the most common criticisms made of the deviancy amplification thesis, namely its inability to establish a causal link between the scale of the problem and the scale of social reaction to it (Jewkes 2004: 75–85), it should be remembered that, according to their recent reformulation by Cohen himself (1972/2002: xxxv), moral panics can still be a very useful tool for studying the perception of risk and moral standards in postmodern societies as long as they are seen as 'condensed political struggles to control the means of cultural reproduction'.

2
A Non-Specific Legal Framework

The law did not devote as much attention to football hooliganism as academia did. In fact, throughout this period, football hooliganism was seen as an ordinary public order problem, the control of which did not require the introduction of specific legislation. In continental Europe, football hooligans faced punishment under the relevant national Penal Code, while in England and Wales they would be charged with a variety of common law and statutory offences contained in Acts that dealt with the protection of public order in general.

The existence of such legislative leniency, however, requires explanation. First, it should be pointed out that it did not denote a lax stance on the part of the social control apparatus. On the contrary, in the UK, where there was a high level of football spectator violence during the period in question, football supporters were subjected to a strict coercive policy, as clearly shown both by the police practices employed when arresting suspects and the severity of the sentences handed down by the courts (Cook 1978; Trivizas 1980, 1981, 1984; Williams 1980; Salter 1985, 1986; Stott and Pearson 2007: 19ff). Second, this widespread attachment to the existing legal framework did not mean that the problem of football hooliganism was negligible or that it was under control. On the contrary, throughout the period football-related incidents spread right across Europe and became increasingly frequent and serious.[1] While retaining the spontaneous, emotional and match-related aspects that characterized them during the 1960s and 1970s, they gradually turned into the expression of organized, pre-planned violence which, depending on the country concerned, involved fairly large groups of football supporters and tended to become dissociated from the match itself. Naturally, this worsening of the phenomenon caused concern among the public and sporting authorities in the countries involved, especially in the UK.[2] Nevertheless, it did not bring about any significant legislative changes.

Lastly, this unwillingness to make any specific legislative response to football spectator violence should not be seen as a by-product of the prevailing perception of what constitutes collective violence in any given society. It would be tempting indeed to assume that the leniency displayed by Italian or Greek legislators, for instance, stemmed from the longstanding violent political conflicts that were a feature of both countries from the 1960s onwards (Crouch and Pizzorno 1978; Graziano and Tarrow 1979; Della Porta 1995; Vakalopoulos 1997; Margaritis and Metaxas 2006). Legislative lenience would thus ensue from the fact that collective violence was viewed as a social banality, thereby revealing a widely shared soft attitude towards groups of deviant youth who were challenging authority. From a different perspective, but following the same reasoning, the leniency shown by Dutch legislators, for instance, would be seen as the natural outcome of the traditionally tolerant stance taken by Dutch society towards all forms of deviancy from social and legal norms (Tash 1991; Downes 1992). Yet, though it may seem plausible to assume that national legislators can to some extent be influenced by the strength or weakness of the security demands emanating from the population, that cannot be the sole explanation for the widespread legislative leniency towards football hooliganism at the time. In fact, despite the climate of rising moral panic (Whannel 1979; Murphy et al. 1990: 73ff) and calls for harsher punishment from sports and political authorities reported in both the liberal and conservative mass media (Tsoukala 1995: 146 ff), the same situation also applied in England.

Far from being isolated or unusual, these demands for security reflected widespread societal anxiety about the state of English youth, which was said to be in moral decline, on the one hand, and, on the other, conservative opposition to the establishment of a decriminalization policy, mainly centred on the introduction of the Children and Young Persons Act 1969 and the Criminal Justice Act 1972, which was expected to result in the collapse of social values and increased juvenile delinquency. A symptom of the profound upheaval experienced by the population as a whole as a result of the decolonization process and the consequent weakening of the UK's role on the international stage, concern about the country's future prompted conservative sectors of the population to resist what they saw as the erosion of moral constraint in an increasingly lax society by launching a campaign to restore law and order. Despite the fact that it was in the context of this campaign that conservatives called for football hooligans, who were seen as representatives of decadent English youth, to be severely punished (Hall et al. 1978: 34–7; Taylor 1982a; Wagg 1984: 212), their demands did not meet with immediate success.

Similar leniency also prevailed at the European Community level where, in spite of the increasing frequency and seriousness of violent football-related incidents during international tournaments, only one Resolution was adopted by the European Parliament in relation to football hooliganism. Passed in 1984, it mainly called for the control of football crowds to be strengthened by enhancing cooperation among all competent state and sports actors (European Parliament 1984). At the European level, while the Council of Europe expressed concern at the growth of violence associated with sport at the local, national and international levels, and called for the drafting of a European Convention to guarantee the introduction of specific legislation in Member States, it still recommended that the issue be addressed principally through education (Council of Europe 1983: D).

Such consistency between the regulation of football hooliganism at both the national level and the EC levels, despite the seriousness of the phenomenon and even the security demands voiced by certain sections of the population, may indicate that there was a common conceptual basis. If so, the widespread adoption of this approach to regulation was arguably influenced by the crime control regime that had predominated in Europe up to then. Widespread since the nineteenth century, this regime, which grew out of functionalist theories on the utility of punishment, was centred on the subjective aspects of offences, that is, the motive and needs of the offender. Associated by several scholars with the dominant role played by the welfare state in dealing with social affairs within industrialized societies and, therefore, with the prevailing idea that individuals who transgress the norm, whether at the economic, social or legal level, should be cared for by the community (Garland 1985; Ewald 1986; Mary 2003), this crime control model not only punished the individual misdeed but also looked to the future by seeking rehabilitation at the individual level and prevention at the collective one. It was widely accepted that, at the individual level, it was possible to exert influence on incarcerated criminals to make them conform to the desired standards of behaviour, that is, to turn them into the 'docile bodies' described by Foucault (1975: 135ff). Moreover, it was this belief in the reforming capacities of disciplinary power which lay behind the rapid spread, throughout the postwar years, of rehabilitation policies for prisoners. At the collective level, it was believed that if the crime rate was to be cut, its structural causes needed to be tackled. The acceptance of this type of causal link, which was supported by many criminologists involved in researching the social factors affecting delinquency (Sellin 1938; Cohen 1955; Merton 1957; Cloward and Ohlin 1960; Sutherland and Cressey 1960; Szabo 1965; Shaw and McKay 1969), had led to the establishment of many long-term social prevention programmes.

In any case, this belief in society's ability to tackle the origins of crime – by changing delinquents and/or the crime-generating aspects of their environment – was based on a series of clear-cut distinctions. First, there was a conceptual distinction between delinquency and deviance whereby it was only the former that could set the criminal justice system in motion. Far from implying that deviance was not being controlled, it meant that responsibility for doing so continued to lie solely with the law enforcement agencies. Second, there was a temporal distinction whereby the criminal justice system could normally be activated only after an offence was committed. Social reaction to an offence was thus ideally seen as a means of preventing laws from being broken, protecting against any further transgressions by the same person and deterring those who might wish to commit similar transgressions. Lastly, distinctions were made with regard to the targets of crime control policies, with social control being mainly directed at criminals seen as threatening to the rest of the community precisely because their behaviour jeopardized one or more of the social values protected by law.

Although, as will be shown below, this crime control policy had been called into question since the 1970s, its rationale continued to determine the regulation of football hooliganism at the national and EC levels until 1985. Consequently, with social control agents still uncertain of what motivated football hooligans, no specific controls were placed on football supporters and they were punished only if convicted of an offence by the courts. Yet at the European level the influence of this policy was clearly on the wane, as illustrated by Council of Europe Recommendation No. R(84)8 on the reduction of spectator violence at sporting events and in particular at football matches, which was adopted in 1984. While recommending the enhancement of coercive policies at the domestic level, the drafters of the Recommendation attached priority to the strengthening of cooperation between the competent state and civilian actors and proposed the introduction of a situational prevention policy, centred on the segregation and surveillance of football spectators. They thus envisaged not only keeping spectators under surveillance and controlling the sale of match tickets, but also erecting barriers to prevent invasion of the pitch and restricting, or even banning, the sale of alcohol inside stadia (Council of Europe 1984: B§4).

Recommendation No. R(84)8 was not binding. Nevertheless, it marked a turning point in the regulation of football hooliganism. For the first time, football hooliganism was seen as a public order problem, the control of which required the introduction of specific measures. The provisions of Recommendation No. R(84)8 denoted a clear departure from the moderate stance that had prevailed at both the domestic and international levels up to then and prefigured the emergence of a new era of social control, based on risk management. It should be noted, however, that situational prevention was already prevalent in the binding instructions issued by UEFA in 1983, which had been drafted in cooperation with the Football Association and the Deutscher Fussball-Bund. It thus seems that, in the case of football hooliganism, change in crime control policy first came about within the private sphere as the result of joint action by sports organizations and public security agencies, and that it was by going down the intergovernmental route rather than the parliamentary one that the revised policy was subsequently drawn up in detail at the international level. In this respect, by providing the justification for the introduction of new public policies, the Heysel tragedy, which is often seen as the single shocking event heralding a new era in the control of football hooliganism in Europe, merely accelerated a change that was already underway.

3
Divergent Policing Styles

The fact that football hooliganism was seen as an ordinary public order problem requiring no special treatment also affected its policing. However, unlike legislative policies, which appeared to be mainly influenced by the rationale behind the prevailing social control model, counter-hooliganism policing policies seemed, in addition, to be determined by territorial criteria, which in turn takes us back to the Europeanization process and the transnationalization of security agencies. In other words, the fact that there were no specific measures for policing football hooliganism during that period was not due solely to the moderating influence the rehabilitation-oriented crime control model had had on the decisions taken by national and supranational legislators, but also to the poor state of police cooperation networks at the European level. Indeed, although Europeanization was already under way and its first effects were visible in the realm of police cooperation (Bigo 1992, 1996), it still had little impact on national police strategies and practices. On the one hand, these early police cooperation networks involved very few actors and, on the other, dealt only with serious forms of criminality such as terrorism and organized crime. Consequently, the policing of football hooliganism remained a national matter which rested on non-specific domestic legal frameworks. Hence, police methods were modelled on the crowd management techniques employed within each country and this resulted in enormous variations.

In countries with a strong parliamentary system and tradition of respect for the rule of law, such as the UK and the Netherlands, whose police forces tended not to be militarized, if at all, and where a low-profile, minimal force strategy was in operation, significant numbers of police only started becoming involved in policing football hooliganism in the 1980s. The importance accorded to protecting public order was thus combined with the need to maintain social peace, which meant that the authorities preferred to seek solutions through consensus, with force being used only as a last resort (Jones 1995: 45; Della Porta and Reiter 1998). It is from this perspective, moreover, that we should view the early situational crime prevention measures that were first introduced in the UK. Their purpose was to keep football supporters under surveillance and control using a variety of devices, ranging from the installation of CCTV systems[1] to measures for keeping football fans segregated both inside and outside stadia.[2] For, even though the widespread use of such measures from the second half of the 1980s onwards cannot be separated from the rapid expansion of a risk-focused crime control model, it needs to be stressed that their initial introduction also had a preventive purpose in that, in addition to trying to bring the conditions that gave rise to reprehensible behaviour under control and improve the effectiveness of police operations, it sought to keep confrontations between football supporters and the police to a minimum.

On the other hand, in countries that had experienced a troubled political history and undergone periods of extreme socio-political violence, such as Italy or Greece, where political demonstrations were often brutally repressed and the security forces had a very poor reputation in the eyes of the public (Della Porta 1995: 58ff; Della Porta and Reiter 1996: 437ff, 1998), the police employed these same methods to crack down on football hooligans. This pattern of policing, whose sole aim was to maintain public order, was thus characterized by the complete absence of any kind of preventive policy and the deployment of ever-growing numbers of police officers, with the chronic shortcomings in police training and equipment being offset by displays of power and numerical superiority (Della Porta 1995: 58ff). Although many criticized this policy, claiming that brutal or belated police interventions often served to trigger or escalate many incidents (Borghini 1977: 36, 48, 57–8; Weir 1980; Marshall 1984; FIGC 1988: 27; Ward 1989: 103), it was only in the second half of the 1980s that changes in the policing of football hooliganism could be discerned.

These national specificities with regard to policing were able to take root and carry on growing all the more easily because, during this period, the progress of international police cooperation was very slow. It had in fact begun in the first half of the 1980s, mainly spurred on by representatives of sporting bodies and UK police forces, but it was still unusual. An initiative launched by the Football Association to establish a network of liaison officers[3] to advise public and sporting authorities abroad in the event that a match involving an English club was to be held in their country was not adopted by other European countries. Although the establishment of this type of international cooperation, which would later serve as a model for the rest of Europe, was part of the extensive internationalization of police work which had been apparent in the UK since the 1960s (Sheptycki 1997), its adoption and promotion by sporting bodies cannot be seen in isolation from the main sporting issue that was then at stake, namely keeping English football clubs in European tournaments. In fact, with UEFA having first considered excluding English football clubs from competitions organized under its supervision as early as 1982, it was out of concern to avoid a ban that the English footballing authorities were pushed into engaging in cooperation and coordinated action to prevent football hooliganism at the international level.

However, this concern only extended to international matches, which were the only ones likely to upset UEFA and result in English football clubs being punished. Consequently, the principle of cooperation was not extended to include preparation for matches inside the country and, throughout this period, the policing of football hooliganism suffered from the same weaknesses in inter-regional and/or inter-service cooperation that were observed in countries with a decentralized police system and/or civil police and military forces with police duties (Erbes et al. 1992). The fact that public security agencies were scattered throughout the country thus continued to foster the rapid development of local practices, make management of services difficult and hamper the transfer of resources, know-how and information, while their institutional proliferation led to increased bureaucratic antagonisms and power struggles. In this respect, there were marked similarities between the policing of football hooliganism in England and the styles of policing prevalent in Belgium, Germany and the Netherlands, where, with the strategies adopted by the many different public security agencies varying significantly from one region to another due to their local nature, their successful implementation was heavily dependent on the prevailing power relations between the myriad police services involved in dealing with the phenomenon.

4

The Social Construction of 'Otherness'

The appearance and rapid escalation of football hooliganism in its modern form quickly attracted the attention of the media which, from the early 1970s onwards, took increasing interest in it. Media coverage in turn became a subject of academic study for the first time but, since such studies mainly focused on the UK press (Hall 1978; Whannel 1979; Pearson 1983; Dunning et al. 1988: 132–56; Murphy et al. 1988, 1990: 96–128), secondary sources on the way the issue was represented in the media elsewhere in Europe are scarce. Consequently, although only covering three countries, namely, the UK, France and Italy, the primary research I have conducted into the quality press coverage from those countries,[1] when combined with existing studies of the tabloid British press, should provide us with a first comparative picture of the subject insofar as it can be seen as representative of the media coverage of football hooliganism during that period, given that it covers one country which had up to then been spared the phenomenon – namely, France – and two countries which had been severely affected by it – one from northern and one from southern Europe.

The following analysis, which seeks to determine the core components of the process through which football hooliganism is defined in the press and assess the media's involvement in legitimating the security apparatus that has been erected to deal with the phenomenon,[2] does not look at the role played by the media in constructing collective identities and/or disseminating ideological schemes among football supporters (Maguire and Poulton 1999a, 1999b; Maguire et al. 1999; Garland and Rowe 1999a; Alabarces et al. 2001; Inthorn 2002; Bishop and Jaworski 2003; Hermes 2005; Boyle 2005; Golfinopoulos 2007). In order to achieve its goals, it starts from the assumption that, far from playing no more than an informational role, the media are actively involved in shaping public debate on social issues, as part of a circle of primary and secondary definers and claims makers through which public problems are socially constructed. Therefore, media coverage of public problems is seen as 'a socially constructed representation of reality and as an arena of problem construction in which struggles to designate and define public problems are waged' (Lawrence 2000: 3). Media discourses on controversial social issues thus become a part of the process whereby public problems are socially constructed, which, on the one hand, involves a variety of institutions and social groups who are all struggling to promote their own values and interests and, on the other, is most effective when it entails the mutual reinforcement of public discourses and policies.[3]

1   A comparison of press coverage across Europe

For practical reasons, it is not possible to look in detail at all the ideological and institutional factors that affect the media representation of football hooliganism. However, by focusing on certain aspects of media coverage of the phenomenon, we can see that there are significant national differences. Schematically, these seem to reflect, on the one hand, the scale of football hooliganism in any given country and, on the other, the meaning accorded to this type of collective violence and to the impact it may have on the well-being of the community. Thus, in France, where football hooliganism emerged in the early 1980s, the issue tended to be addressed only when football-related incidents occurred abroad. Seen as the manifestation of a distant problem that was rife among football supporters from other countries, such incidents, which were reported only if they exceeded a certain level of seriousness, were usually described briefly, in a neutral tone, without using sensationalist language or making any value judgements about football hooligans.

By contrast, given that the phenomenon was already widespread in the UK and Italy, journalists in those countries accorded it a great deal more importance, as demonstrated in particular by the rise in the number of articles devoted to the issue. In Italy, football hooliganism was reported relatively widely as soon as it appeared there in the mid-1970s. This was not the case in the UK, however, where, even though it had existed since the mid-1960s, it did not attract wide media coverage until the 1970s because, as pointed out earlier, until then journalists had tended to disregard pre- or post-match incidents and/or to minimize the gravity of the incidents they did report (Taylor 1982a: 71–2; Murphy et al. 1990: 115–17).

Analysis of the mounting media attention given to football hooliganism in the two countries also reveals other differences. In Italy in the 1970s, journalists tended to filter news according to its importance and to report only the most serious football-related incidents (De Leo 1988: 286; Broussard 1990: 109), which were usually presented in neutral terms, devoid of any value judgements or pejorative assessments. In the UK, on the other hand, the increase in the level of coverage given to football hooliganism involved engaging in a process of constructing threat by employing several of the typical methods for doing so. Thus, journalists started reporting all football-related incidents, even minor ones, thereby giving an impression of ever-growing disorder, which in turn was likely to fuel an atmosphere of insecurity.

This repetitive reporting of 'incidents', which, mainly consisting of a series of self-fulfilling prophecies, was an integral part of a deviance amplification process (Cohen 1973; Hall 1978; Whannel 1979; Taylor 1982a), was not necessarily due to a desire on the part of journalists to espouse a particular political position. It also reflected the effect of working routines on the production of news since, when operating to tight deadlines, journalists will often write their stories by rehashing existing articles on the same subject (Neveu 2004: 72ff; Marchi 2005: 144). However, presenting the news in this way had an enduring effect on the representation of football hooliganism because, among other things, it gave rise to a mental scheme into which all future incidents would subsequently be fitted in order to make full sense of them. The general climate of insecurity thus created in turn ended up amplifying the scale and effect of such incidents, thereby helping to justify the initial scheme later and establish a conceptual framework whose use was increasingly hard to challenge, even when the latter was not backed up by the facts. Thus, football-related incidents that broke out abroad were invariably attributed to English football supporters even when it turned out that they were the victims rather than the aggressors (Whannel 1979; Williams et al. 1984/1989:168).

2   Football hooliganism in the British press

The British quality press did not use the quasi-military sensationalist rhetoric which at that time began to characterize coverage of the phenomenon in the tabloids.[4] However, while continuing to report the facts soberly, it began to criticize the failure to crack down adequately on football hooliganism. Although bellicose terms were not often used to describe the behaviour of football supporters, the idea that the government had to 'make war on football hooligans' was already current in 1969 (Dunning et al. 1988: 152). In the 1970s, calls for the existing law to be strictly enforced and for the counter-hooliganism apparatus to be strengthened frequently featured in both conservative and liberal newspapers (*The Times*, 5 January 1976: 2; *Guardian*, 30 July 1975: 1, 25 November 1976: 8). The penalties imposed on football hooligans were deemed so inadequate that, in the early 1980s, even liberal-minded Members of Parliament were demanding that custodial sentences be imposed more frequently (*The Times*, 3 February 1983: 12), thus echoing the increasingly strong pressure being exerted by the press (*The Times*, 2 March 1984: 4). As Ian Taylor has rightly pointed out (1982a: 49), such calls were heavily reliant on the mounting levels of media coverage of football hooliganism since they conformed to the rules of a cycle of stimulus and response where each new incident was seen as evidence of the need for a new initiative, which was almost invariably described as an efficient clampdown liable to obviate the need from more severe measures.

Appearing against a background of societal anxiety arising from decolonization, as mentioned earlier, these calls for a more stringent crackdown on football hooliganism mainly reflected the desire of certain sections of the population in the UK to redraw the contours of their society by setting the law up as a real and symbolic barrier to disorder – a social disorder which not only stemmed from recent political disorder but also, and above all, heralded the future decline of the country. While young football supporters were seen as the incarnation of this disorder and, as such, began to incur the wrath of an increasingly large part of the community, demands for increased security encompassed not only football hooligans but also other groups of working-class youth (Hall 1978; Whannel 1979; Taylor 1982a). The use of deliberately unruly and occasionally violent behaviour by such groups, be they teddy boys, skinheads or football hooligans, within a peaceful society which valued self-control as well as respect for law and order was thus viewed as particularly threatening and in need of a firm response precisely because it was at odds with the dominant values of that society.

At the same time, these calls for a tougher crackdown on football hooligans would not have been effective if they had not been backed up by many public discourses that sought to construct 'otherness' – a preliminary stage to, and necessary condition for, successfully implementing a repressive policy against any social subgroup. As has often been shown, constructing social enemies is a common reaction of communities undergoing internal crisis since, as a result of its opposition-based definitional scheme, it enables the community in question to retain its internal cohesion by (re)defining itself as a value system (Foucault 1961; Becker 1963; Erikson 1966). The threat of disorder embodied in various deviant groups is thus posited as being both a measure and a tool with which the community can be defined – as opposed to an ideal order based on the prevailing norms of beauty, virtue and truth (Kearney 2003: 29). Nevertheless, these social enemies can only be effectively excluded from the community to which they belong if they are subjected to a severing process whereby a clear line can be drawn between the perpetrators of the allegedly threatening acts and the rest of the community (Girard 1972; Edelman 1988). This process, which is always involved in establishing guilt (Peelo and Soothill 2000: 134), allows, moreover, all moral ambiguity to be removed from both the coercive measures to be adopted against the wrongdoers and the social values thus defended. Once established and legitimated in the eyes of the population, the exclusion of these social enemy figures makes it possible for a series of coercive measures, ranging from control tools and practices to detention, torture and even death, to be imposed (Foucault 1975; Hall et al. 1978; Cohen 1972/2002; Goode and Ben-Yehuda 1994; Critcher 2003). Furthermore, the binary logic on which their exclusion depends is a useful hegemonic device because it allows complex issues to be simplified. With the 'other' set up as the 'hyper-signifier of all that is bad and immoral' (Lazar and Lazar 2004: 239–40), the complex causes of his/her actions are hushed up, thus ensuring that no possible blame can be attached to mainstream society.

In the case of football hooliganism, this severing came about through the way in which the social profile of football hooligans and the causes of their behaviour were represented. It took place at a number of levels but was much more prevalent in the tabloids. Football hooligans were thus subjected to a dual severance, at once cultural and biological, which gave the impression of multiple pathology. The stigmatization of their divergence from the dominant modes of behaviour, as demonstrated by the frequent use of terms such as 'thugs' or 'yobs', was accompanied by the stigmatization of their divergence from mental health norms. In the latter case, they appeared to be fundamentally different from other individuals because their behaviour was devoid of any rationality. Such irrationality might be the result of the consumption of alcohol by 'louts, whose sense of moral values, invariably soaked in alcohol, ha[d] sunk to the lowest human depths' (*The Times*, 15 March 1985: 30); it might also reflect the inferior intellect of young people described as 'twits' (*Sunday Mirror*, 28 September 1975)[5] or 'mindless morons' (*Daily Mirror*, 4 April

1977);[6] lastly, it could quite simply be seen as pathological, with football hooligans being called 'lunatics' (*The Times*, 16 March 1985: 1).[7] In any case, football hooligans were viewed as being particularly threatening, specifically because of their alleged mental deficiencies, which made their behaviour unpredictable and thus difficult or even impossible to control. In this respect, anxiety was fuelled by the spectre of a form of behaviour that reflected the murky depths of unconscious aggressive impulses, reminiscent of an original disordered state which, either individually or collectively, could only be brought under control through the use of reason (Tsoukala 2006b: 373–4).

Rooted in a society which was otherwise deemed healthy precisely because it was enlightened by an awareness that was supposed to ensure self-control, football hooligans might profoundly disrupt the established order of that society, tarnish its founding principles and regularly contaminate it with their irrational behaviour which, what is more, might be contagious. It was hardly surprising, therefore, that sometimes they ended up being compared to a real social cancer – a comparison which considerably aggravates the threat because, over and above the seriousness of the illness to which it refers, it calls to mind the tendency for tumours to spread, the uncertain outcome of any treatment, the permanent risk of relapse and, lastly, the possibility that the cancer in question is incurable. Describing football hooliganism as a 'cancerous growth lying within the body of society' (*The Times*, 15 March 1985: 30) thus makes it clear that it is imperative to adopt whatever measures might be necessary to protect the body in peril, with the seriousness of the danger justifying the potentially extreme nature of any such measures as well as any side-effects they might have. It is worth stressing here that the consequences of establishing such a picture of irrationality are not limited to justifying the security measures to be adopted. Since, by definition, any possibility of sensible communication between football hooligans and the rest of the community is ruled out, all social prevention policies are rendered useless and the adoption of security measures becomes the only possible response to a social threat of this nature.

This severing effect was further reinforced through the dissemination of two other images which in a way complement each other: one of savagery and one of bestiality. While, in the first case, 'outbursts of savagery' by football hooligans (*The Times*, 16 March 1985: 1)[8] clearly distinguished them from the rest of supposedly civilized society, the plethora of animal-related metaphors and rhetorical figures that appeared especially in the tabloids, and in which football hooligans were, for example, compared to animals that should be caged (*Daily Mirror*, 21 April 1976),[9] set them apart once and for all from the human race. According to the image thereby projected, football hooligans were particularly threatening because their standards of behaviour were closer to those of the animal kingdom than those of so-called civilized humanity.

The finishing touches were put to this severing of football hooligans from the rest of society by presenting them as stereotyped figures, who were completely detached from their socio-economic milieu and devoid of any individual or collective trait that might have given them some kind of social substance. Apart from the occasional press article connecting football hooliganism with the low social position of its perpetrators (*The Observer*, 15 October 1972: 27), discourse on the causes of the phenomenon tended either to content itself with rather simplistic approaches, attributing it to the breakdown in family discipline or postwar urban reforms, or stick solely to considering it within the sporting domain, linking it to poor refereeing or the increasingly exorbitant wages paid to football players.

Having been subjected to a binary representation which, in divesting them of any social substance, reduced them to a two-dimensional image, these 'cartoon' figures which, furthermore, supposedly operated outside of any kind of rational action framework, were clearly cut off from the rest of the community. From then on, the only ties English football hooligans had with their society stemmed from the disorder they caused within it and their ability to sully the international image of the country, which they were said to shame and disgrace (*Daily Mail*, August 1980).[10] Given that these ties were indisputably negative, there was also an overwhelming need to protect the community by adopting whatever control measures were presented as being appropriate for that task.

3   Football hooliganism in the Italian press

Reflecting the ranking of values and political priorities within a society in any given period, media representation of football hooliganism was markedly different in Italy. Though faced with a phenomenon that was in several respects comparable to that which existed in the UK, the press did not resort to creating moral panic about football hooligans. It steered clear of constructing stereotyped images not only by usually adopting neutral patterns of representation, but also by examining in detail the causes of the phenomenon. Thus, while recognizing that football hooligans went to matches 'with the intention of causing trouble' (*La Stampa*,

12 January 1976: 12), journalists had no hesitation in attributing such violence in part to referees, coaches and football players by pointing to the role they played in triggering conflict (Borghini 1977: 42).

In emphasizing the emotional aspect of the behaviour of football hooligans, this wider causal approach did not simply broaden the range of actors seen as responsible for such violence. It also looked at the background against which such violence was being generated, examining both the socio-political context and the socio-cultural characteristics of football hooligans. The phenomenon was thus often attributed to psychological factors connected with the marginalization and frustration felt by young people or the pressure put on them by their peer groups, socio-political factors related to the crisis affecting social institutions, or even cultural factors arising from young people's need to belong to subcultural groups (De Leo 1988: 291–2). In all cases, this violence, the origins of which were rationally identifiable and contextualized, was seen as relatively limited in scale. The tendency was therefore to downplay its significance in Italy and to stress that, far from being 'a sadly unique Italian phenomenon...in many other European countries...incidents were far more serious and frequent' (*Corriere della Sera*, 13 January 1976: 24).

The position adopted by the Italian press to football hooligans cannot be understood outside of the social and political context of the time. Beset by fierce internal conflict, Italian society was undergoing socio-political upheaval throughout the 1970s. In this climate of widespread social violence, in which the attention of the public was primarily focused on the threat posed by Italian terrorism, football-related incidents were of concern only if they overstepped a certain level of seriousness (De Leo 1988: 288–9). Likewise, since it was accepted that the tendency for many young people to join extremist and often violent political groups, or even terrorist groups, had a certain rationality that ought to be scrutinized so that the underlying conflict could be resolved, the public, when all was said and done, found it uncontroversial for football hooliganism to be included among these types of youth violence and for similar explanatory frames to be applied to it.

Of course, the fact that this was the prevalent approach did not mean that there were no calls for order to be restored. The authorities were thus expected to control the phenomenon effectively (Borghini 1977: 44). However, such demands for security were not the same as those that featured in the British press. First, in most cases they did not call for the immediate adoption of security measures and, second, they did not imply unconditional acceptance of police interventions which, on the contrary, were often viewed as brutal, ineffective and even unjust (De Leo 1988: 293).

This type of coverage, which predominated throughout the 1970s, began to change considerably in 1979 when one supporter died as a result of football hooliganism. This change, which became clearly identifiable during the subsequent period, not only reflected the worsening of the phenomenon but also, and above all, the evolution of Italian society. In a climate in which social peace and socio-political stability were gradually being restored, the political class dissociated itself from any form of collective violence, whether it emanated from student circles, the labour movement or minor political groups. The violence of football hooligans, which from then on was an isolated social phenomenon, thus became a concern and quickly ended up being seen as highly threatening to the well-being of the community (Marchi 2005).

Part II
Blurred Boundaries (1985–97)

Introduction to Part II

Following the Heysel tragedy, football hooliganism began to capture the interest of a growing number of researchers from several different European countries. The plethora of studies published during that period are testimony to the great vitality of the academic community which, as well as taking up existing theories, went on to explore new epistemological avenues. However, far from leading to the formulation of broad explanatory frames that were sufficient to clarify the many different facets of the phenomenon, curiously this vitality ended up weakening the position of the academic community as a definer of football hooliganism.

This paradox was due mainly to the angles from which European scholars chose to examine the subject which, in turn, appeared to be closely bound up with developments within British academia as well as the power relations that existed between the latter and other European researchers. In fact, in the overwhelming majority of cases, this profusion of studies looked solely at the behaviour of football hooligans, either in isolation from, or in correlation with, its sporting or socio-political context. The role played by other actors, such as security agencies and sports authorities, and the interplay between them and the world of the football supporter were thus neglected in favour of a search for aetiology which, despite appearances, remained one-dimensional. While this fascination for a single facet of the phenomenon reflected the personal choices of the researchers involved in this definitional process, it also stemmed from the controversy which had, through its own momentum, surrounded debate, initially in the UK alone but later in other countries also. Although British academics still played a dominant role within Europe, they had become deeply divided as a result of disagreements between different schools of thought which, by carrying several foreign scholars along in its wake,[1] was unwittingly holding back research from looking at other facets of the phenomenon and making it practically impossible to develop and advocate explanatory frames capable of achieving widespread acceptance. As Frosdick and Marsh rightly pointed out (2005: 78), 'more time [was] devoted to demolishing the views of other "experts" than to developing alternative explanations'. Since this flawed polyphonic chorus was seen, or at least presented, as evidence that it was impossible to establish an academic definition of the phenomenon,[2] the definitional power from then on lay in the hands of social control agents and thus became inextricably tied in to the processes by which football hooliganism was controlled. On the other hand, in the few countries, such as Belgium, where the academic community was able to hold on to its definitional authority, scholars were able to participate in those processes and flag up their repressive tendencies.[3]

In the absence of a single, overarching definition of football hooliganism in Europe, social control of the phenomenon would develop against a background marked by the Heysel tragedy, as well as by the swift emergence of a crime control model based on actuarial risk management, rapidly accelerating Europeanization and a growing politicization of security issues. From then on, football hooliganism was seen as a very serious public order problem, control of which required the adoption of specific laws and policing policies. The emergence of a paradoxical legal specificity at the national, EC and European levels thus went hand in hand with the growing convergence of policing strategies and practices, as shown in particular by the introduction of numerous proactive control measures which were extremely detrimental to civil liberties.

During this period, in countries where football hooligans were already widely portrayed as dangerous, that picture continued to prevail and tended to replace the lenient discourse prevalent elsewhere, thus becoming the standard representation of the phenomenon throughout most of Europe. Based on certain discursive schemes employed when constructing social enemies in general, public discourses on football hooliganism turned violent supporters into a genuine social threat by divorcing them completely from their historical context and depriving their actions of any rational foundation, thereby justifying whatever steps might be taken to deal with the phenomenon as long as they were seen to be effective.

5
The Vibrancy of the Academic Community

1 Psychological theses

In the late 1980s, the theory of ritualized violence and the quest for social status gained ground among researchers in the UK (Ingham 1989) and influenced the work of scholars elsewhere. Taken up in France by Michel Raspaud (1990), it was also developed in Italy by Alessandro Salvini (1988) who, as well as adopting its main points, supplemented it by pointing to patterns of domination–aggression and the search for identity/group membership. According to Salvini, football hooliganism was the symbolic expression of domination behaviour which, though not entirely ritualized, derived from belonging to a group of football supporters and the status that this conferred on young people who were going through an identity crisis. He also saw it as being closely bound up with many situational variables, ranging from the architecture of stadia to the rules and values of sporting events, specific forms of group behaviour and the highs and lows of matches.

Another Italian researcher, Alessandro Dal Lago, used these same elements to explain the phenomenon. Carrying on from the work of Marsh, he took the view that, in most cases, the violence employed by football hooligans was of a symbolic nature since it manifested itself mainly through gestures, insults and chanting. On the rare occasions when this descended into actual violence, it was due partly to an established tradition of enmity between rival gangs of football supporters and partly to certain situational parameters linked to the progress of the match (Dal Lago 1990a; Dal Lago and Moscati 1992; Dal Lago and De Biasi 1994).

The situational approach, also taken by Anthony King (1995), prevailed too in the work carried out by a Belgian research team who, starting from the principle that in certain contexts individuals lose their free will, attributed the phenomenon mainly to the crowd situation, the violent nature of football as a spectacle, flawed policing, the physical environment, the consumption of alcohol and the ideological beliefs of the supporters (Dunand 1987; Rimé et al. 1988; Leyens and Rimé 1988).

In the 1990s, psychological studies focused increasingly on certain factors that were believed to exacerbate football hooliganism. In one of these, Bruna Zani and Erich Kirchler (1991) laid particular stress on strong identification with the football club, academic failure and the group effect. In the Netherlands, Hans van der Brug (1990, 1994) concluded that football hooliganism could not be dissociated from the breakdown of parental authority and the high level of academic failure among young violent football supporters. Such behaviour therefore demonstrated, above all, the crisis that contemporary societies were undergoing as a result of the crumbling of value systems and the traditional forms of social control.

Reflecting the importance given since the 1980s to situational approaches in theories concerning the analysis and management of crime and security in postmodern societies (Clarke 1995; Shearing 2001), the idea that football hooliganism is associated with a whole series of situational variables raises a number of problems. First, even though it has the virtue of underlining the role that many different situational factors may play, by focusing on these it ends up denying the personalities of the actors themselves. The behaviour of football hooligans is no longer seen as the outcome of a conscious decision, but as the product of many different impersonal parameters which, if only they could be altered, would be sufficient to bring about the desired change in behaviour.

The limitations set on the explanatory scope of determinist approaches as a result of their inherent reduction of reality were well illustrated by the findings of the research conducted in Greece in the late 1980s by Christos Tsouramanis (1988). According to Tsouramanis, although it was possible to establish some significant correlations between outbreaks of violence and the existence of certain factors likely to precipitate such incidents,[1] these were not sufficient in and of themselves to explain the phenomenon, which remained largely a random occurrence since it relied on human initiative.

Similar reservations were expressed a little later by Gerry Finn (1994) who, based on his studies of Scottish football supporters, believed that the phenomenon could not be explained without looking at the psychological state of the actors. In his view, football hooligans were, first and foremost, teenagers looking for thrills that might also provide them with a sense of belonging, of *communitas*. Participating in violence thus played a unifying role within the group, with each young man having to overcome his own fears before developing the social qualities required for the cohesion of the group and being able to commit himself to it and acquire the desired social identity.

The psychology of the actors also drew the attention of John Kerr (1994) who, applying Michael Apter's reversal theory, saw football hooligans as young men looking for satisfying and fulfilling experiences that would emphasize their masculinity. Perceiving the outside world in terms of a struggle for power and control, they would tend to dissociate themselves from conventional societal rules and expectations concerning behaviour and engage in activities that were likely to bring them immediate gratification.

2   Anthropological theses

In the UK, Gary Armstrong returned to the thesis that actual violence was rare among football supporters and advanced the idea that the latter were principally engaged in constructing individual and collective identities by seeking exciting entertainment and experiences that would enable them to reach, or even exceed, their personal and social limitations. In such a carnivalesque atmosphere, it was only as a result of changes in policing and the representation of the phenomenon in the media that violent incidents became frequent and serious (Armstrong and Harris 1991; Armstrong 1994, 1998; Armstrong and Hobbs 1994; Armstrong and Young 1997).

Being one of the few theses to draw attention to the significance of the interplay between football supporters, security professionals and the media, this theory remains very important. However, the criticisms made of all the theses centred on symbolic violence still apply because it too underestimates the scale and seriousness of actual violence. It also suffers from the same methodological weaknesses as the anthropological theses already mentioned because, by confining itself to very limited fields of enquiry, it cannot be seen as being applicable beyond the local level.

The work of Alain Ehrenberg in France (1984, 1985, 1986, 1991) did not encounter such problems because its starting point was completely different. According to his theory, which was developed in the mid-1980s, football hooligans were socially vulnerable young men who were ensnared in the contradictions of the consumer society and the business world. Starting from the premise that all sporting events embody the ideal of equality in our democratic imagination, he saw football hooliganism as the outcome of a brutal clash between the democratic ideal of sport and the reality of the socio-economic exclusion young football supporters were experiencing. Their desire to attain the contemporary individualist dream, which, in order to achieve the greatest possible success, pushes everyone to be an actor in their own lives rather than a spectator in the lives of others, prompted them to choose the football stadium as the preferred field of action because, given its extremely high media profile, it gave them the chance to become visible and, as a consequence, to acquire the social identity they so desired.

By linking the emergence of football hooliganism to the changes that had taken place in Western societies as a result of the increased influence of consumer values in the private sphere and business values in the public sphere, Ehrenberg was the first French scholar to put forward a coherent interpretation of the phenomenon. It was well received and rapidly taken up by other researchers so that the idea that the quest for social visibility was a key motivation for young football supporters/members of contemporary individualist societies was regularly included in many subsequent studies on the causes of football hooliganism (Comeron 1996: 58; Bromberger 1996; Le Noé 1998: 62).

The indisputable interest of this theory should not, however, mask its limitations because, just as we shall see later with regard to the criminological theses, it only applies if football hooliganism is actually present. It is, in fact, impossible to reverse its logic and argue that, when there is little or no football hooliganism in certain parts, or even the whole, of a particular country, the socio-economic and cultural conditions which supposedly determine the emergence and development of the phenomenon are absent or do not operate in the same way. Furthermore, given that Ehrenberg's theory focuses on football hooligans' desire for media coverage, its application is also time-limited since it quite obviously does not include the current behaviour of certain hooligans who do the complete opposite and engage in pre-arranged fights that take place as far as possible from public gaze.

Also in the 1980s, another French researcher, Christian Bromberger, returned to the ritualized violence thesis, but put forward an explanatory frame for football hooliganism that was much broader than the ones advocated by the psychologists and anthropologists mentioned earlier. While stressing the eminently symbolic nature of such violence, which rarely degenerated into action, he attributed it to a quest for personal accomplishment and recognition, typical of the members of any youth subculture, as well as to the development of a genuine spirit of sporting militancy. Exhibited at the level of language, organization and types of behaviour, this sporting militancy furthermore formed part of a competitive logic that mirrored the one in action on the pitch, with groups of football supporters competing fiercely to impose their hegemony in the stadium and assert their legitimacy as the rightful representatives of all young supporters. While this type of parallel competition could be traced back to the agonistic model of sporting competition, it also satisfied young football supporters' need for visibility by allowing them to put forward non-sports-related demands, especially those connected with defence of a local identity and/or a political ideology (Bromberger 1984, 1996, 1998; Bromberger et al. 1987).

Far from minimizing the level of actual violence, Bromberger linked it to the ways in which football supporters' groups organize themselves. In doing so, he reiterated the distinction usually made between English and Italian models of fandom[2] in order to argue that in countries where the Italian model prevailed, namely Italy, France and Spain, the institutionalized forms of fandom created stable bonds of sociability and interdependence which helped to control, prevent and even curb any shift into actual violence. On the other hand, in the countries of Northern Europe where the English model, characterized by the ephemeral nature of football supporters' groups, prevailed, the forms of social bonding were not strong enough for patterns of internal control or a division of responsibilities to develop.

The importance Bromberger attributed to the specificities of the shift into actual violence undoubtedly shields him from the criticisms made of most of the psychological and anthropological studies already mentioned. However, linking the way football supporters organize themselves to their involvement in actual violence is not without problems. First, it has to be said that, throughout the 1980s and 1990s, violent incidents were much more frequent and serious in Italy than Bromberger would have us believe (Roversi and Balestri 2000: 186; Louis 2006: 71ff). Second, his theory scarcely applies, if at all, in Greece, Portugal or Turkey, for example, where the supporters of big football clubs are organized into structured groups but are also regularly involved in incidents of violence, in football as well as in other sports (Courakis 1988, 1998; Koukouris et al. 2004; Koukouris and Taxildaridis 2005; Marivoet 2002; Ünsal 2004; Erkiner 2004). This therefore again suggests that the shift into actual violence cannot be explained solely by the meaning individuals assign to their behaviour, thereby disregarding any consideration of the various elements that go to make up the social identity of individuals and the many different social, political and economic factors that are likely to directly or indirectly influence their behaviour.

Furthermore, despite its undeniable role in helping us to understand the behaviour of football supporters, the introduction of the notion of militancy as a means of explaining their actions[3] is of limited value because it has not been properly developed at the theoretical level. In fact, this idea, which seems to have emerged from observations made in the course of numerous field studies, hardly exceeds the level of description because, paradoxically, though borrowed from political science, it has not been related to political science studies on collective action and militancy. The fact that Bromberger seems not to have taken account of the work done on the subject by authors as diverse as Mancur Olson (1965), Albert Hirschman (1970), Anthony Obershall (1973), Charles Tilly (1986) and Daniel Gaxie (1997) has without doubt deprived his thesis of further rewarding exploration that would have shed new light on the issue.

3   Sociological theses

The sociological theses developed during this stage are mainly macrosociological and cover a wide range of disciplines, borrowing elements from political sociology, subcultural studies and the sociology of deviance.

3.1   Theories based on political sociology

Although no British researchers pursued Taylor's thinking in their attempts to explain football hooliganism, his work was very influential abroad, not so much as a theory for interpreting the phenomenon but as an analysis of the historical context within which such collective violence appeared. Reflections on the role played by the changes made to the structure of football throughout the postwar years were thus included in the explanations of the phenomenon proposed by authors as diverse as Antonio Roversi in Italy (1990: 89), Günter Pilz in Germany (1996), Manuel Comeron in Belgium (1996) and Patrick Mignon in France (1998).

At the same time, a new theory founded on political sociology appeared in France. From the 1990s onwards, advocates of the critical theory of sport (Vaugrand 1999) sought to interpret football hooliganism from a Marxist perspective, but their starting point was distinctly different from Taylor's. Seeing sport as an ideological state apparatus, in the Althusserian sense of the term, the main representative of this school, Jean-Marie Brohm (1993, 1998), considered football to be a political, economic and ideological superstructure of advanced capitalism that exacerbated the agonistic logic of the actors and contributed to widespread social disintegration. As such, it incorporated multiple forms of violence, ranging from various types of embezzlement and corruption to doping and football hooliganism. Consequently, the footballing spectacle was simply a catalyst for forms of violence that were generated and fuelled by the event itself.

While having the merit of sweeping aside the usual high-minded discourse on the benefits of sport, this interpretation of football hooliganism, which derives from a view that is scornful of the virtues of sport in general (Escriva and Vaugrand 1996; Redeker 2002; Brohm 2002; Brohm and Perelman 2006),[4] is wanting in several respects. First, it continues to reduce reality because it is trapped within its own ideological limits. In other words, by vastly over-exaggerating the negative aspects of football, it repeats the mistake it has criticized in others, namely, that of conveying a supposedly universal picture of the world which is in fact only the product of a particular ideology shared by certain social groups. Furthermore, the fact that it is rooted in the holism of Marxist ideology prevents it from assigning the individual an important place within the historical process described. Football hooliganism is therefore seen as an abstract form of behaviour that is the result of the different material dynamics operating within a society in which the individual has a mechanical rather than an organic role. This interpretation of social reality is all the more problematic in that it relies on no field studies to confirm, redraft or invalidate its initial hypothesis. In the absence of any systematic study of the manifestation of football hooliganism and/or the factors affecting its emergence and subsequent development in many different European countries, this theory seems therefore to fall into the category of ideological construction rather than rigorous analysis of a social phenomenon.

3.2   Subcultural theses

The theory, developed earlier in the UK, that football hooliganism could be attributed to an age-based subculture was reprised in this period by the German scholars Erwin Hahn (1989) and Kurt Weis (1990), who saw such behaviour as a quest for identity and social prestige during adolescence and post-adolescence. However, since most German football hooligans were not of working-class origin, the emergence of such a subculture there was believed to be a reaction to the absence of excitement and thrills in the daily lives of young people who, growing up within a very ritualized milieu, were inclined to adopt behaviour, such as the displaying of Nazi insignia, that was provocative both at the symbolic level and in reality. In Italy, the subculture theory was mainly adopted by Antonio Roversi (1986, 1990, 1991, 1994) who, while echoing Taylor's view of the role played by the changes that had taken place in football during the postwar years, saw in groups of football hooligans a kind of masculine subculture which quickly took root because, on the one hand, it could give the members of such groups a positive identity, based on prestige and peer recognition, and, on the other, it was fuelled by the traditional enmity that existed between different football supporters' groups, mainly due to the political allegiances of their members.

By emphasizing the age factor and, as a consequence, teenagers' need for identity, these works highlight what is most probably one of the keys to understanding the phenomenon. However, these approaches also reduce reality in that they ignore a whole series of parameters that go to make up the personalities of these teenagers, ranging from their social position to their standard of education and even their criminal background. This partial view of the actors is all the more problematic because it dissociates them from the social milieu in which they operate, thus disregarding all factors relating to the actual functioning of security agencies and/or sporting bodies, as well as all the political, economic and bureaucratic factors that may very well have an influence on such behaviour.

From the mid-1980s onwards, the concept of a delinquent subculture was also taken up by a team of researchers headed by Eric Dunning (Williams et al. 1984/1989; Dunning et al. 1986a, 1986b, 1987, 1988, 1991; Dunning 1994, 1999, 2000). Here, however, it was not the age of the football hooligans that was emphasized but their social origin. Armed with the conclusions of their research, which showed that English football hooligans mainly came from the lower strata of the working class, these scholars, who adhered to what they called the figurational current of sociology,[5] asserted that football hooliganism was the product of a subculture of male violence which was typical of all social relations involving people from those sections of society and acted as a substitute for the status and social gratification that were denied to working-class youth. Taking from the work of Norbert Elias on the civilization process (Elias and Dunning 1986) as well as from Gerald Suttles

(1968), they used the notion of ordered segmentation (a term coined by Suttles), to explain the role played by age, gender and territory in the formation of peer groups when faced with opposition or conflict from the outside. Football hooliganism was thus a working-class reaction that was broadly similar to the reactions members of that class would have to any kind of threat, the tendency to resort to violence being facilitated by the fact that working-class youth, precisely because of their social origin, had never learned to exercise the self-control expected of them by the rest of society and saw physical confrontation as a source of identity, status, meaning and exciting entertainment. Given that this familiarization with aggressive behaviour went hand in hand with a certain degree of homogeneity in working-class experiences,[6] football hooliganism manifested itself at football grounds because they constituted a cultural terrain that was conducive to the semi-institutional establishment of satisfying masculine identities.

By highlighting the cultural relationship between the manifestation of football hooliganism and the social origin of its actors, Dunning and his team, like others, helped to situate the phenomenon within a rational socio-cultural framework. However, this relationship only sheds light on the ways in which the behaviour of football hooligans is shaped and expressed, leaving the reasons for the emergence and current scale of the phenomenon largely unexplained. For, while it is probably true to say that many cultural elements that are peculiar to the British working class are intrinsic to the way football supporters behave, the causal link between this observation and the emergence and subsequent expansion of football hooliganism is flimsy in several respects.

First, as Beatrix Campbell and Adam Dawson have pointed out (2002: 70), Dunning's team addressed the question of gender only as an epiphenomenon in what was essentially a class-based analysis, focused on the notion of ordered segmentation.[7] However, given that this notion in turn relies on the existence of a subculture of violence, it is important to remember that the subculture of violence theory has never been empirically and irrefutably proved (Robert and Faugeron 1980: 94–100; Rosner Kornhauser 1984: 187–9). On the contrary, researchers have often concluded that there is no meaningful correlation between belonging to a lower social class and participating in violent activities (Ball-Rokeach 1973: 747). So to see the working class as a class that structurally generates social disorder simply echoes the old mantra 'labouring classes, dangerous classes' (Chevalier 1958), which, despite repeatedly featuring in public discourse, has no solid academic foundation (Armstrong 1998: 303–6).

Furthermore, the argument put forward by Dunning and his colleagues suffers from the same limitations as the theories of Taylor and Clarke mentioned earlier in that it too relies on the social origin of English football hooligans for its claims. It is therefore open to the same criticisms with regard to its applicability to other European countries affected by football hooliganism. One of the first people to call into question the supposed general applicability of this theory was Herbert Moorhouse who, in light of his research into Scottish football hooliganism, concluded that the explanation offered by Dunning did not apply to Scottish football hooligans (1984: 309–10). The same reservations were later expressed by researchers from both the UK and other countries. Those from the UK included Alan Bairner, who shed light on the inter-communal nature and politico-religious foundations of football hooliganism in Northern Ireland (Bairner and Shirlow 2001; Bairner 2002), and Richard Giulianotti, who, taking up Moorhouse's arguments, clearly showed that the violent behaviour of Scottish football supporters was not the product of social factors but of a set of historical and cultural factors tied in with their religious beliefs and their (re)positioning vis-à-vis English football hooligans (Giulianotti 1991, 1995; Giulianotti and Gerrard 2001). The researchers from outside the UK included myself, Antonio Roversi, Carlo Balestri and Gabriele Viganò, who stressed the mixed social composition of Italian football hooligans (Tsoukala 1995; Roversi and Balestri 2000; Balestri and Viganò 2004), Serge Govaert and Manuel Comeron (1995), who explained that Belgian football hooligans were not mainly of working-class origin, Gabriel Colome (1997), who linked football hooliganism in Spain to longstanding rivalries between different regions of the country rather than social factors, Nikos Peristianis (2002), who showed that Cypriot football hooligans came mainly from the middle classes and attributed their behaviour to political factors and the emergence of local identities, and Ramon Spaaij (2006, 2007), who stressed the diverse social origins of Dutch football hooligans.

Despite these limitations, this theory enjoyed widespread circulation which, while bringing swift international fame to its authors, also left them exposed to a growing number of criticisms. Having initially vehemently rejected these (Dunning et al. 1991; Dunning 1994), Dunning eventually relativized his conclusions on the universality of his explanation (1999, 2000) without, however, calling into doubt the validity of his theory which, on the contrary, he sought to confirm through international collaboration (Dunning et al. 2002). From then on, standing by the crux of his initial theory on the subculture of masculine violence, he contended that the way in which football hooliganism manifested itself was subject to what he called fault lines, namely, an array of nationally-based cultural and structural factors.

It should, nevertheless, be noted that this endeavour suffered from a certain lack of objectivity, with Dunning tending to criticize and rapidly relativize the impact of any works that argued against his thesis while attempting, on the contrary, to take credit for any conclusions reached by works which seemed to fit in with his own. Thus, he failed to answer the criticisms about whether his theory concerning the UK was applicable elsewhere and, although he recognized the validity of some of the foreign works that stressed the mixed social composition of football hooligans in other countries, he did not put them into perspective. Furthermore, the use Dunning made of foreign works whose theories fitted in with his own was superficial because he confined himself to picking up on any mention of the working-class origin of football hooligans without considering what were sometimes significant differences in the condition of the working class in each country. Hence he based his theory on the supposed homogeneity of working-class conditions across Europe, regardless of the duration and scale of industrialization, labour market patterns during the twentieth century or the political and socio-cultural evolution of the countries concerned. Yet it is precisely these factors which determine the relative position of the working class within a society, as well as the perception its members have of that position and the eventual emergence of certain standards of behaviour that are peculiar to them. Lastly, other works cited by Dunning as explicit confirmation of his thesis posed serious methodological problems. Such was the case, for example, with the work carried out during the 1990s by a team of Greek researchers under the direction of Antonis Astrinakis (Astrinakis and Stilianoudi 1996; Astrinakis 2002). In fact, though admitting that they had been unable to collect any data on the social origin of the football hooligans studied, the researchers concluded that the young men in question were of working-class origin by assuming that, since their study had been conducted in a working-class area, it was unlikely not to be the case.

3.3   Theses founded on the sociology of deviance

The work of Stanley Cohen, which had been developed during the previous period, came to exert an ever-growing influence both in the UK and abroad (Dunning et al. 1988: 132–56; De Leo 1988; Murphy et al. 1990: 96–128). The constructivist approach was further boosted in the

1990s when Gary Armstrong broadened its scope, which, prior to that, had been confined to the media, to encompass law enforcement agents (Armstrong 1994, 1998; Armstrong and Hobbs 1994; Armstrong and Young 1997). Armed with his ethnographic observations, he emphasized the role that public security agents could play in constructing social problems for political and bureaucratic purposes. From this viewpoint, football hooliganism, once it had become the subject of moral panic, could be used by the media and public security agencies as justification for boosting the social control apparatus, on the one hand, and adopting certain forms of policing, such as undercover work, electronic surveillance and intelligence-gathering, on the other.

Despite their pioneering character and the unquestionable interest they represented for understanding such a complex social phenomenon, these studies were of limited importance because they remained essentially descriptive. In fact, though carrying on from the work done by Hall and Cohen on the construction of social problems, Armstrong failed to support his conclusions with a solid theoretical base founded on constructivism and/or studies on the sociology of organizations. In the absence of a properly developed theoretical frame, his remarks on the role of security professionals are left wanting and do not allow us to grasp their full social and political meaning.

4   Criminological theses

This period saw the appearance of the first criminological studies, which were conducted in Belgium in the second half of the 1980s. Their principal representatives, Lode Walgrave and Kris van Limbergen, took their inspiration mainly from the work of Albert Cohen on the delinquent subculture (1955), Travis Hirschi (1969) on the impact of certain social bonds on the decision whether or not to engage in crime,[8] and of Richard Cloward and Lloyd Ohlin (1960) on the role certain economic and social circumstances can play in influencing an individual to turn to crime. Combining elements of these theories with the findings of their empirical research, Walgrave and van Limbergen saw football hooliganism as behaviour that was typical of young men from the lower social strata who, having had negative experiences of social institutions, realized that their social prospects were poor and sought to compensate for their societal vulnerability by joining cultural subgroups that might provide them with the identity and excitement they desired. Having explained the social origin of the phenomenon in this way, they went on to attribute the shift into violence to the coming together inside football stadia of many different factors that were conducive to it. In particular, these included the consumption of alcohol, crowd anonymity, the fact that the holding of games on a regular basis fostered the establishment of a mass tradition, and the interest shown in such young people by the media, thus giving them the social visibility they sought (Limbergen et al. 1987; Walgrave and Limbergen 1988, 1990; Limbergen and Walgrave 1992).

While resembling the explanations offered by subcultural studies, the thesis put forward by these scholars was different because for them the decision to engage in crime depended on a whole series of socio-economic, cultural and situational factors within which the social position of the actors, while of vital importance, in and of itself was not sufficient to explain the emergence of the phenomenon. By seeking to be comprehensive, this theory did indeed offer one of the most complete explanations for football hooliganism in that it was based on factors that were both internal and external to the actors, with the external ones also being linked to the socio-economic environment in general and the sporting context in particular. Nevertheless, despite its indisputable merits, this interpretation of football hooliganism only applies in the event that the phenomenon is present. In other words, just as in the case of Ehrenberg's work mentioned earlier, the logic of this theory cannot be reversed since the infrequent appearance and even absence of the phenomenon in certain European countries does not mean that the conditions the authors see as providing the framework for the emergence and development of football hooliganism are present in any lesser degree or nonexistent. This is the case, for example, for most regions of France as well as southern Italy where, despite the existence of a large socially vulnerable youth population, there has been relatively little incidence of the phenomenon so far.

Inspired by the work of Walgrave and Limbergen on the social vulnerability of football hooligans as well as Robert Merton's work on anomie (1957, 1964), in the early 1990s, I decided to move away from examining the factors affecting the development of football hooliganism and look at the conditions that gave rise to it (Tsoukala 1995). By studying the situations in England and Italy, I confirmed that there was a link between the vulnerable social position of young football supporters and their violent behaviour since I found that football hooligans were young males from different social backgrounds but whose position on the social ladder was similarly low. Thus football hooligans seemed to be young men who, as a result of rising anomic frustration, were predisposed to aggressive behaviour (Berkowitz 1962), the triggering of which was partly attributable to the convergence within stadia of certain situational variables (Debuyst 1974), such as the anonymity of the crowd and the decreased fear of punishment when taking action with their peer group. Wishing, nevertheless, to go beyond this deterministic approach, I also took account of fluctuations in space and time and of the ways in which football hooliganism was manifested, as well as the meaning that the socio-cultural aspects of football matches might have for football hooligans. Thus, on the one hand, I established a link between the emergence of the phenomenon within one country, or certain regions of it, and the degree of economic crisis affecting that country or its regions, or, at the very least, the relative degree of frustration felt by young people living in those areas; on the other hand, I bore in mind the fact that, given the frequency of games and the high level of media coverage given to them, football stadia had become ideal platforms from which to broadcast any social or political demands football supporters might have. I asserted, therefore, that football hooliganism tended to appear in countries that were undergoing socio-economic crisis and that it had an air of protest about it that was all the stronger if the domestic traditional movements of social protest were failing in their task. From this perspective, football stadia were venues for expressing social malaise, while the ways in which the phenomenon manifested itself varied according to the socio-cultural model that prevailed in each of the countries studied.

Although this theory has the merit of separating out the factors underlying the emergence of football hooliganism from those that influenced its subsequent development, the idea that football hooliganism is connected with putting forward certain kinds of political demands outside of the classic channels of social protest is far from indisputable. Even though admittedly an increasing number of works have pointed out that football stadia have become places of political protest, this phenomenon is usually associated with either authoritarian or totalitarian governments, calls for independence or the expression of extremist political beliefs (Ramonet 1990; Boniface 1998, 2002: 28ff; Sack and Suster 2000; Vrcan 2002; Čolović 2007). Yet, if we accept that football stadia can, where necessary, act as political platforms for subsections of the population who are denied access to decision-making and news broadcasting centres, we also have to accept that, given that the first football hooligans came from underprivileged social milieux and suffered from similar forms of exclusion, football stadia could have served the same function for them also. Otherwise, we are denying such young men a political identity.

However, this assertion raises numerous problems with regard to the question of defining social movements and social actors, a subject that has created deep divisions within academia. In France, for example, these divisions have become focused on two schools of thought. According to Alain Touraine (1978), who has influenced, among others, François Dubet (1987) and Michel Wieviorka (1998), a social movement is one in which the actors are engaged in protest action in order to call into question the established order and control the forces of development within society. For such protest action to be called political, it must also borrow the vocabulary, main issues and repertoire of action that typify the political field. Other kinds of collective action that fail to obey the rules of the political game make no political sense.

This interpretation of social reality has, however, been challenged by a number of recent studies into the forms of action employed by the inhabitants of underprivileged French suburbs which, while shedding light on the intrinsically political nature of urban riots characterized by the emergence of new forms of collective action, point to the systematic public discrediting of any mobilization of socially disaffiliated young people which does not fit into the categories that prevail within a given political field (Bonelli 2003; Kokoreff 2003). By refuting the idea that analysis of the functioning of social life may be reduced to a series of indicators that are implicitly taken to be invariable, these scholars believe that denying members of a social group, when acting outside of the formal political realm, the ability to produce a representation of themselves in the symbolic struggles over division of the social world leaves the way clear for other representations. These representations, which may be political, institutional, media and even academic, thus portray such delegitimized mobilizations in emotional or instrumental terms and, having dispensed with the power relations that shape the production of social and legal norms, are able to impose such images through the reinforcement of social control and 'normalizing' social structures (Bonelli 2003: 23).

6
Paradoxical Legal Specificity

It is undeniable that the Heysel tragedy, which was broadcast live on several European television channels, left a deep impression on people's minds and transformed the way in which football hooliganism had been perceived up to then by public authorities across Europe. The footage of the dying victims, which was replayed constantly on television just as, many years later, that of the terrorist attacks of 11 September 2001 would be, made the dangerousness of the phenomenon so clear that it left no room for doubt that an appropriate legal framework was required to control it. This gave way to a period in which football hooliganism acquired a certain degree of legal specificity.

Given earlier trends, it is not surprising that such legal specificity should have first appeared at the European level, with the adoption in 1985 of the European Convention on Spectator Violence and Misbehaviour at Sports Events and in particular at Football Matches (Council of Europe 1985). Drawn up in the aftermath of the Heysel tragedy, the Convention did not provide any genuinely new policies since it essentially reproduced the main provisions of the Council of Europe Recommendation referred to in Part I (Tsoukala 1995: 213ff). Consequently, it attached priority to the enhancement of domestic and international cooperation among all competent public agencies and sports authorities[1] and called for the implementation of a situational prevention policy, still centred on the segregation and surveillance of football spectators. From that point onwards, however, the policy in question was extended in terms of time – to cover the periods before and after fixtures – in terms of space – to cover places outside of football stadia – and in terms of its target population – to cover potential troublemakers and people under the influence of alcohol or drugs (Council of Europe 1985: art. 3).

As far as this last point was concerned, the European Convention differed significantly from the earlier Recommendation, the provisions of which applied solely to known troublemakers. In so doing, it allowed the control of deviance to become institutionalized for the first time. This highly unexpected stance on the part of an institution whose *raison d'être* is to protect human rights was further developed by UEFA in the 1985 guidelines drawn up in collaboration with an expert group from the Council of Europe (Taylor 1987: 644), which also permitted security measures to be taken against potential troublemakers. From then on, social control was not confined to dealing with the actual harm caused by criminal acts, but extended to address the potential threat posed by deviant behaviour. Law enforcers could thus profile suspects for being part of a disorderly rowdy group, drinking (or being drunk), using offensive/vulgar language, making obscene gestures, standing up too often in the football ground, and so on. Social control became increasingly anticipatory, with assessment of the potential dangerousness of football supporters left to the discretion of public and private security agents, who were free to set and amend the criteria used to subject individuals to an ever-growing control apparatus.

This expansion of social control coincided with demands for tougher punishment for football hooligans. The states that signed up to the European Convention were thus entrusted with the task of ensuring that appropriate penalties or administrative measures were applied to those found guilty of offences related to football violence (Council of Europe 1985: art. 3c). Actually, it was this call for more stringent coercive measures that gave rise to all subsequent counter-hooliganism laws, the main purpose of which was usually to ensure enforcement of the European Convention at the national level. Varying significantly from one country to another in terms of their number, content and date of enactment, these counter-hooliganism laws, which were further bolstered with numerous specific measures contained in legislation with broader scope, ended up giving football hooliganism a certain degree of legal specificity. Examination of the key definitional elements put forward by European legislators shows that incriminating behaviour consisted of a) the employment by one or more persons at, or in connection with, a sporting event of abusive acts or words that involved the use or threat of violence and caused harm to a person, damage to property or a breach of the peace; and b) ordinary acts that merited punishment if they were committed at, or in connection with, a sporting event.[2]

The creation of such a specific legal framework for dealing with football hooliganism had a significant effect on the control of football spectators in that it entailed the introduction of special measures and new sanctions. Of the former,[3] the most important included the banning of alcohol inside and around football stadia in the event of high-risk football matches, the use of various surveillance devices inside and outside football stadia, and the preventive detention of potential troublemakers. Of the new sanctions,[4] the most significant was the imposition of domestic and international football bans. Although, as will be seen later, these measures and sanctions meant the setting in place of a control apparatus that was extremely detrimental to civil liberties, their adoption did not attract any particular criticism because they were presented as appropriate ways of addressing the seriousness and newly acquired legal specificity of the phenomenon that needed to be tackled.

Yet this legal specificity remained paradoxical because it was developed in the absence of a proper legal definition of football hooliganism. In fact, the phenomenon was broken down into a set of punishable behaviours that occurred at, or in connection with, sports events and, in particular, football matches. Therefore, the spatial criterion became not simply the key definitional element of football hooliganism,[5] but also led to the introduction of a new aggravating circumstance whereby people who committed offences in connection with sports events were subjected to harsher penalties than those who committed similar offences in other circumstances, thus institutionalizing earlier judicial practices (Cook 1978; Trivizas 1980, 1981, 1984; Williams 1980; Salter 1985, 1986).

The adoption of this type of analytical approach, which calls to mind the difficulties encountered by jurists in the course of their many attempts to define organized crime (Blakesley 1998; Ottenhof 1997: 45–8), suggests that football hooliganism is a commonsensical notion that can only be used as a generic term.[6] This inability to translate such an empirical notion into legal terms raises problems when it comes to drawing a clear dividing line between legality and illegality, as well as for the political marshalling of the many different types of order that characterize contemporary societies (Albrecht 1997: 19ff) and the ensuing role played by individuals in the ongoing renegotiation of the power assigned to the social control apparatus. In other words, while some types of behaviour were clearly covered by the law,[7] the legal definition of certain other types of behaviour that were on the fringes of (il)legality, in a grey area consisting of deviant rather than delinquent acts,[8] was heavily reliant on the discretionary power of public and/or private security agents. This could therefore vary greatly from one context to another, depending on the service to which the security agents in charge belonged, their grade and even their mood (Bayley 1985; Monjardet 1996; O'Neill 2004, 2006), the level of risk allegedly associated with the fixture and the prevailing crowd control methods used in a given context (Adang and Cuvelier 2001; Stott 2003), thereby creating an area of legal uncertainty. The vagueness of the definition of public order, and thus what constituted a breach of it, jeopardized not only what would ideally be fair implementation of the law in a given territory, but also the protection of civil rights and liberties. The resultant weakening of the principle of legality in turn weakened the principle of proportionality and, in some cases, the principle of accountability applicable to social control agents. As the phenomenon to be controlled was not clearly defined by the legislator, public and private security agents were able to incorporate a potentially infinite series of behaviours into their sphere of activity. It was possible for control and surveillance devices to be developed without assessing whether they were suitable for dealing with the key elements of the behaviour in question or proportional to the threat posed to security by the transgressors. This potentially unlimited extension of the social control realm left targeted populations very vulnerable because the blurring of the boundaries between legality and illegality meant that the sphere within which they could live their lives beyond the gaze of social control agents was not clearly defined.[9] It also made it practically impossible for the intrusive power of security agents to be challenged. Contrary then to the appearance given by the fact that many laws had been enacted at the national level, the legal framework surrounding football hooliganism was in reality determined by the executive rather than the legislature, thereby leaving football spectators exposed to the arbitrariness of the social control apparatus.

Furthermore, the fact that the executive played such a dominant role in regulating football hooliganism meant that, of the values requiring protection, priority was given to people and property. This was the objective sought by all the special laws, be they preventive or repressive, passed during most of the period in question. By contrast, democratic order, which was being violated by the increasingly frequent occurrence of racist behaviour inside football stadia, was not recognized at the national level as an important value in need of protection until the 1990s,[10] and it would take more than a decade for it to be recognized at the EU and European levels. Although in 1994 the European Parliament had invited the European Commission to fight against all forms of racism and xenophobia in a sports context (European Parliament 1994), it was not until 1999 that the European Commission sponsored FARE, the first EU-wide anti-racist football network. At the European level, the Council of Europe adopted a Resolution on the prevention of racism and xenophobia in sport only in 2000.

1 The politicization of security

It was not only in the context of combating football hooliganism that security came to be afforded such primary importance; it was also high on the European political agenda during this period, especially after 1989 (Waever 1995; Anderson 1996; Buzan et al. 1998; Palidda 1999; Mary and Papatheodorou 2001; Bigo 2002; Lagrange 2003: 53ff). Indeed, concerns had been raised since the mid-1980s about what was perceived to be a general upsurge in disorder, mainly stemming from the increasing pace of Europeanization, the end of the Cold War, the growth of transnational migratory movements, globalization, the rise in environmental and food insecurity, and the tremendous technological and scientific advances that were taking place. These changes, which occurred over a relatively short time span, gave rise to heightened tensions around identity, worries and fears of many kinds and a general deep anxiety about anything that could be seen as triggering or escalating the disorder that already existed. Believing that order and security, allegedly weakened by all these changes, needed to be protected at all costs against anything that might further undermine them, the political classes throughout Europe quickly moved internal security matters to the top of their agendas.

This politicization of security was seen by some scholars as being one of the main consequences of the weakening of sovereignty (Anderson 1996; Mary 2001; Bigo 2002) several of the key elements of which became impaired or even disappeared as a result of the changes mentioned above.[11] They therefore believed that the more states withdrew, as a consequence of the deregulation of political and socio-economic life, the more they would expand the social control realm in order to demonstrate their legitimacy (Houchon 1996: 82) as the guarantors of security within their borders. Since the task of safeguarding property and people fell within one of the few areas of political action whose effects had not been weakened by Europeanization, it therefore became a major political issue. It allowed politicians to retain their image as decision-makers/regulators in the realm of social matters by assuring the electorate that they were able to act at the local level, bring the harmful effects of disorder under control and even establish new points of reference specifically because the social control apparatus had been strengthened. This focusing of politics on security would thus bring about a form of governance which, being unable to provide reassurance to the population during this period of transition, was based on the management of fear and insecurity. Linking this politicization of security with the widespread dissemination of the security-related discourses employed by both politicians and journalists, the upholders of discursive approaches to security also highlighted the fact that, since the end of the Cold War, the focus on security had originated mainly from a political process of threat construction, which they coined securitization (Waever 1995; Buzan et al. 1998).

Far from emanating solely from the needs of political actors, this transforming of security into a major political issue had also come about as the result of new calls for social protection from the social strata most affected by the above-mentioned changes, whose anxiety in the face of the weakening of the institutions that had up to then protected their social rights made them demand increased security in other areas of their social lives. Calls for security thus showed not only a sense of being members of a group that deserved to be protected by public actors, but also a desire on the part of members of society to restore or rebuild social links both among themselves and between themselves and the state (Palidda 1999; Lagrange 2003: 53ff). The increasing power of such calls throughout the period in question therefore served to justify the political process that was taking place elsewhere, thereby creating a network of interlocking policies which reinforced and legitimized each other.

2   A new perception of threats to security

One of the key features of the politicization of security has been the redefining of both security threats and the target of social control along two distinct but interconnected lines, arising from the end of the Cold War and the emergence of the risk society respectively. In the case of the former, the vacuum left by the disappearance of the Soviet enemy swiftly gave way to a new perception of the threat to security which, freed from the earlier political connotations, saw criminals as constituting the main danger to the internal security of European countries. This replacement of the political threat by the threat of crime had been underway since the mid-1980s when numerous official reports and public discourses on internal security issues sought to define threats by establishing a close association between various deviant and criminal behaviours, ranging from terrorism and organized crime to illegal immigration, juvenile delinquency, petty crime, urban violence and football hooliganism. With the end of bipolarity, this process gathered pace and expanded so that the threat itself became magnified. The main feature of this change was the rapid spread of the idea of a European-wide security continuum (Bigo 1996) focusing on the very existence of any threat to the internal security of European countries, regardless of the actual danger it posed or its legal status. From then on, threats were deemed to be interconnected and deterritorialized since, given their supposed transnational nature, they could no longer be exclusively external or internal. Consequently, they were subject to a dual process of definition. On the one hand, their outer boundaries were not clearly delineated, thus making it easy for them to become part of a broader set of disparate threats. On the other hand, their inner core, following the gradual introduction of its constituent parts into the sphere of criminal law, had become increasingly specific, thus leaving no possible room for doubt that they should be seen as security threats. For example, while several aspects of illegal immigration were gradually criminalized, the issue itself was also linked to many different (trans)national criminal phenomena, ranging from organized crime to petty crime and urban violence. In other words, each of the phenomena included or to be included in the security continuum simultaneously became both a specific threat, as a result of the criminalization or harsher punishment of some of its features or even the gradual incorporation of some of its deviant facets into the social control realm, and, in the absence of any delimitation of the threat itself, a general threat. The parallel development of these two sides of the same process gave the social control apparatus potentially infinite opportunities to expand under the pretext of efficiently protecting internal security in Europe.

3 Risk and crime control

The establishment of this twofold definition of security threats was greatly facilitated by the rise of postmodern risk societies which, according to Ulrich Beck (1992), went from being preoccupied with wealth production itself to being concerned with eradicating any sources of risk that might jeopardize the latter. As is widely acknowledged today, concern with risk and the ensuing introduction of strategies for coping with it have had a profound impact on the design and implementation of crime control policies.

This led to the strengthening of an earlier trend first seen in the 1970s, namely, the tendency to amend the crime control model and, as a consequence, redefine the targets of social control.[12] By pointing to the poor success rate of rehabilitation programmes (Martinson 1974), US neo-conservatives were the first to call for reform of the rehabilitation-oriented crime control model and to advocate the introduction of a realistic social control policy based on the constant reassessment of benefits and costs (Feeley 2003: 118ff). In so doing, they denied the relevance of any causal link between crime and the social environment and focused solely on the idea of controlling the social effects of crime (Wilson 1975). These ideas spread to Europe with the coming to power of neo-conservative governments. Consequently, they made their first appearance in the UK where the development of a new crime control model formed part of the neoliberal policy of freeing individuals from dependence on social welfare (Crewe 1989; Reiner 2000; Feeley 2003: 123ff). Abandonment of the principle of rehabilitation thus became an integral part of a general process of profound changes in social control which, furthermore, led to drastic cuts in the funding of the welfare state and the privatization of many public services. It should be pointed out here that this focus on risk did not in fact result in the abandonment of a rehabilitation-oriented crime control policy. Instead it allocated new meanings to existing approaches and practices to make them consistent with the risk-based way of thinking (Shearing 2001: 212). Therefore, while, formally speaking, certain measures were still based on the earlier crime control model and others followed the risk-focused one, the risk-based mindset had been gradually taking over (Hörnqvist 2004: 39).

The rationale behind this risk-focused crime control policy ran counter to the earlier policy in many respects. First, its main objective, to protect the community against all risks to its security, removed the distinction between deviance and delinquency. The social control apparatus was no longer seeking to defend the community against a danger posed by the commission of an offence, but to protect it from the potential risk inherent in a given behaviour. As soon as it became possible to mobilize the social control apparatus to protect against risk rather than danger, its sphere of activity could encompass both delinquent and deviant behaviour, even if it meant removing the latter from the remit of the social services which had been responsible for dealing with it up to then. Hence control of deviance was no longer a form of social control that had veered off course, but a key component of the legal system which could not be dissociated from the way in which crime control policies actually operated. In fact, that shift calls into question the whole concept of the criminal justice system in a democracy. The institutionalization of the control of deviance is so wide-ranging that it can no longer be seen as a specific swing away from a liberal social control apparatus to one that is more authoritarian in orientation. It is no longer a question of occasional deviations by a criminal justice system that otherwise complies with the rule of law, a subject that was analysed at length in the 1980s (Delmas-Marty 1983: 102ff). The hold the social control apparatus increasingly exerts over the private sphere is now formally established and legitimized. Indeed, while human rights defenders saw this 'legal upgrading' of the control of deviance as a symptom of the continual redefining of power relations between the executive and the people or the (re)positioning of public and private actors within the political and security fields (or both), the executive refused to admit that it was jeopardizing civil rights and liberties. The assumption that the law, as a set of rules relating to what is due to the community rather than to individuals, sought to protect the common good (Bastit 1990: 370) was used to justify the expansion of the social control apparatus as a necessary adaptation to a new context on the grounds that the security of democratic regimes was being protected against all current and future risks (Tsoukala 2004a, 2006a). At the same time, it should be stressed that merely expanding the social control apparatus beyond the limits established by democratic governments is not in itself sufficient proof of the emergence of an authoritarian state in the strict sense of the term. No matter how serious they were, the infringements of civil rights and liberties that resulted from this reconfiguration of the relationship between citizens and the law did not radically alter the basis of political order in European countries (Tsoukala 2004a). What they did reveal was a profound change to the basis of the legal order in a democracy, which has been permanently enlarged to include normative proposals originally advanced within an extralegal normative order (Leben 2001). This eventually led to the relinquishing of one of the key elements of the rule of law, namely safeguarding individuals from the arbitrariness and overarching power of the state apparatus.

In another respect, as the risk-focused crime control policy departed from the rehabilitation principle, it put aside its former attachment to the notion of individual and collective guilt. It was no longer a question of dealing with individuals by focusing on the subjective aspects of their actions or the social factors that might determine their behaviour. Accepting these parameters as being non-reversible, the social control apparatus no longer sought to change the past or transform the future by rehabilitating criminals and/or altering their crime-generating environment (Simon 1997; Shearing 2001: 209). From then on, it focused on anticipating and controlling the effects of socially undesirable behaviours. In other words, by introducing crime management policies that sought to combat the symptoms rather than the causes of crime, belief in the reforming capacity of society had been replaced by a quest for social comfort.

The spread of this new philosophy had a considerable impact on the institutions responsible for crime management. First, retreating from the notion of guilt meant that the social institutions in charge of managing crime-generating factors had become marginalized in favour of the police who, by definition, were the only institution authorized to assess and manage crime risk. Second, focusing on controlling the effects of socially undesirable behaviours had changed the nature of punishment. Prison was no longer a punishment in itself, accompanied by an element of rehabilitation, but a tool for neutralizing unruly individuals and preventing them from harming the rest of society. This new function of imprisonment inevitably caused an exponential increase in the number of inmates, the majority of whom came from the lower social strata, leading several scholars to see it as a means of controlling populations on the basis of class (Melossi and Pavarini 1981; Garland 1985, 1996; Wacquant 1999a; Sainati and Bonelli 2000/2004; Mary and Papatheodorou 2001) and/or colour (Agozino 1997; Webster 1997; Lévy and Zauberman 1999; Mucchielli 2001; Esterle-Hedibel 2002), or even as a means of developing regional economies (Christie 1994; Pratt 2001).

This risk-focused crime control policy was also contingent on a radical change in target. It was no longer directed at individual offenders but at members of alleged risk-producing groups. Therefore, it went beyond the commission of actual offences to encompass the potential behaviour of members of deviant groups. Yet this shift from the individual to the collective level jeopardized the foundations of democratic legal frameworks, which relied, on the one hand, on the principles of legality and personal liability and, on the other hand, on the relationship between the offender and the individual or collective victim (Shearing 2001: 208). More explicitly, the claim by social control agents that they had some kind of overall knowledge of future behaviours denied people the freedom to decide whether, and under what circumstances, they would commit any given act, denied them the possibility of having the act in question morally assessed so that liability and thus punishment could be established, and, finally, denied the role of the victim in justifying punishment. From then on, the random nature of the elements that went to make up the three-way relationship of offender–offence–punishment was put aside in favour of a deterministic vision of the world which, in searching for certainties, ended up blurring the boundaries between ordinary and punishable behaviour. Since danger was an individual concept while risk could only be a collective one, the social control apparatus no longer sought to punish offenders because of the dangerousness of their actions, but to control certain groups within society according to how serious the risks they supposedly posed to the community were perceived to be (De Giorgi 2000; Shearing 2001; Silver and Miller 2002). The control of these groups thus adhered to the proactive principle of actuarial risk assessment, while the choice of target population reflected the outcome of the struggle over the definition of security threats going on within the political and security arenas at any given moment, which in turn reflected the values and interests of all the groups of actors involved in the process. Once the proactive principle of actuarial risk assessment prevailed, its implementation meant the introduction or development of various types of security measures that created a continuum of control (Feeley and Simon 1992: 459) encompassing individual offenders, potential individual offenders and even individuals who had no *a priori* connection with the behaviour being controlled. In this continuum of control, surveillance and intelligence-gathering quickly came to the fore (Lyon 1994, 2001, 2004; Fijnaut and Marx 1995; Norris et al. 1998; Jones 2000; Gill 2000; Dillon 2003; Graham and Wood 2003; Bonditti 2004). In the case of football hooliganism, for instance, CCTV cameras installed in football stadia monitored the behaviour of troublemakers, rowdy football supporters and ordinary football fans alike, while the gathering and exchange of intelligence extended well beyond known and potential troublemakers to include even ordinary football supporters wishing to attend international tournaments. The establishment of this continuum of control was, furthermore, greatly facilitated by the apparent depoliticization of these tools which were presented as being neutral scientific and, by extension, apolitical mechanisms. The disguising of the political functions of this new form of social control under the cloak of science was well explained by Eric Silver and Lisa Miller, who pointed out that actuarial risk assessment tools tended to depoliticize the process of social regulation they sought to implement precisely because they were not 'designed to explicate and alter the causes of violence and recidivism but instead to identify risk markers that best predict them' (2002: 144).

Nevertheless, the ensuing infringements of civil rights and liberties were not merely a consequence of this continuum. They were, above all, the product of the very rationale that lay behind the risk-focused crime control policy. Indeed, since the legal protection of civil rights and liberties was, by definition, focused on the individual (Weinreb 1987: 129ff), the fact that the group rather than the individual was now the main target of social control could only mean that the scope of this protection, which to a certain extent no longer had a purpose, was seriously weakened. In other words, the framework for the legal protection of freedom was still based on the individual approach associated with the principles of the earlier rehabilitation-oriented policy, while the framework for risk-based social control had gone on to adopt a collective approach which, in the absence of any similar such provisions in the human rights realm, significantly weakened the position of those who came up against the social control apparatus.

This vulnerability was further reinforced by the removal of the earlier temporal and spatial limits. Risk-based social control was potentially boundless in that it could range from a definite *post*-offence period to a vague *ante* risk behaviour period and from a clearly defined area of illegality to a sphere of activity that may well encompass unspecified areas of private life. Its changing relationship with time and space eventually altered its relationship with reality insofar as it focused on potential rather than actual behaviour. Thus its effects were being generated not only because of its links with actual reality, but also through its extension into virtual reality. Social control agents, far from confining themselves to containing offenders, were seeking to control ill-disciplined individuals through the advance management of risk-producing groups, whose behaviour was monitored by making predictions about where and when it was likely to appear (Bigo 2008). In doing so, they abandoned the old reactive patterns of action, which had been circumscribed by spatial–temporal criteria and other specific characteristics of offenders, and adopted a proactive approach, namely one that was active and free from the earlier constraints, allowing them to become the quasi-absolute definers of both the spatial–temporal parameters and the methods of action to be employed, regardless of what the individuals in question may have actually done.

Yet, despite seeming to adhere to the risk-focused principles that at that time governed the perception of threats and the establishment of measures for tackling them, the structure of the new social control model seemed at variance with the individualist nature of postmodern neoliberal consumer societies. In fact, while the dominant economic models and cultural norms in Western societies were increasingly focusing on the individual, social control was moving away from that reality and turning towards virtual reality, which disregarded the actual nature of the individual in favour of focusing on the potential nature of the group as risk-producer. Of course, this approach is consistent with the collective properties of actuarial risk predictions, which are designed solely for use with groups. At the same time, it has to be said that this 'unreal' attribute of social control was simply a product of the transfer to the field of disciplinary power of the dematerialization that had already taken place in the economic domain (Néré 1989), where actuarial risk management tools had come from. However, although the economic origin of the new social control model may explain its virtual and collective nature, it does not explain why politics adopted this model, which in some ways ran counter to prevailing social norms. Nevertheless, if we turn the question round and put politics at the heart of the reasoning, we see that, in the postmodern era, it has been the functioning of politics itself which has been sliding towards virtual reality. According to Beck, in societies that are defined less and less by structures and more and more by processes, political discourse is dematerialized and becomes projected towards a future that is defined by scenarios so that action taken in the present regulates events that have not yet happened. In an increasingly fluid world, deprived of permanent structures, action taken in the present can no longer rely on the rapidly disappearing existing framework or modify its constantly changing features. Its points of reference and effects are thus displaced into the future and shaped by scenarios that are projected from the present in order to colonize the future (Beck 1999: 52, 2002: 40). Instead of being mere suppositions with a precarious hold on reality, these scenarios embody a part of reality (Beck 1999: 139) insofar as they effectively transform the future, which is thereafter seen as the cause rather than the effect of action taken in the present. Where football hooliganism is concerned, the introduction of football banning orders 'on complaint' in the UK as well as various administrative football bans in other European countries illustrate this point well. The construction of security problems around specific scenarios (Rasmussen 2002: 332ff) by politicians and security agents alike and the immersion of disciplinary power in virtual reality have thus brought the field of politics and that of security, as well as, *in fine*, the criminal justice field, together around a common perception of reality. Consequently, the new social control model only appears to run counter to individualist norms because its focus on the collective does not stem from any kind of axiological position, but is a corollary of its entrenchment in a virtual world.

In the case of football hooliganism, this concurrence of views between politicians and security professionals, however strong it may have been, was mainly confined, throughout that whole period, to the level of national politics and its European extension, namely the Council of Europe. In other words, the principles inherent in risk-focused crime control policy had still not been taken up very widely at the EC level, as shown by both the relatively late adoption of risk-based policies by EU institutions and the continuing attachment of European parliamentarians to a rehabilitation-oriented crime control policy. In the case of the former, it should be pointed out that, given that they were not legally authorized to directly regulate sport-related issues,[13] EU institutions have long opted for indirect methods that make it impossible to discern the ideas underlying them.[14]

The influence of the risk-based mindset first became apparent in the Council Recommendation of 22 April 1996 on guidelines for preventing and restraining disorder connected with football matches. It recommended making an overall assessment of the potential for disorder and standardizing the exchange of intelligence about known or suspected groups of troublemakers (Council of the EU 1996: II.1). One year later, the Council Resolution of 9 June 1997 on preventing and restraining football hooliganism through the exchange of experience, exclusion from stadia and media policy confirmed this position by recommending that football bans imposed on known and suspected troublemakers should also apply to football matches in a European context (Council of the EU 1997: §1). This Resolution is also a good illustration of the increasing influence of the risk-based mindset, which had moved beyond institutionalizing the control of deviance to altering the very thought processes of decision-makers. Indeed, despite the fact that there was no evidence to suggest that an international network of football hooligans existed, the Europe-wide belief that internationally linked criminal networks posed a deterritorialized threat drove its authors to ask for the annual compilation of national reports on the activities of international networks of football supporters' groups (Council of the EU 1997: §2).

Yet this Council position was not shared by the European Parliament, which remained attached to the principles inherent in rehabilitation-oriented crime control policy. This was clearly shown in its Resolution of 11 July 1985 adopted immediately after the Heysel tragedy. Members of the European Parliament, while complying with some of the policies contained in the 1985 European Convention in that they too recommended the strengthening of coercive and situational preventive measures (European Parliament 1985: §1–3), took a distinctly different stance in specifying that security measures should be applied to known troublemakers only (European Parliament 1985: §3e). They also diverged from the European Convention by calling for the development of a long-term preventive policy for combating the social and political causes of the phenomenon (European Parliament 1985: C, §7, 10, 11). In other words, while agreeing that in order to tackle football hooliganism effectively the relevant security policies needed to be strengthened, they rejected any institutionalization of the control of deviance and refused to dissociate the phenomenon from its social context.

This position was further confirmed in the Resolution of 22 January 1988. On the one hand, the enhancement of international police cooperation and the establishment of a European-wide network for collecting and exchanging intelligence recommended in the Resolution were not meant to apply to suspected troublemakers. On the other hand, football hooliganism was linked to numerous economic, political and social factors, such as the fuelling of nationalism and xenophobia by the mass media and the influence of far-right political organizations (European Parliament 1988: E, G). This strikingly broad definition of football hooliganism[15] was also of interest because of the way it prioritized social values. In opposing the stance taken by the Council of Europe and the Council of the EU in this way, the European Parliament was the only European institution to show concern about protecting both public and democratic order in Europe and put forward appropriate measures for doing so (European Parliament 1988: §6, 15). Reiterated in the 1990 Report of the Committee of Inquiry into racism and xenophobia, the 1994 Resolution on the EU and sport and the 1996 Report on football hooliganism and the freedom of movement of football supporters, this stance in favour of the protection of democratic principles and the rule of law led to repeated public condemnations of racism in football stadia. It also gave rise to increasing concerns about the arrest and deportation of football supporters solely on the basis of suspicion, as well as confirmation of the principle that the security apparatus should not be used against suspected troublemakers.

7
Convergent Policing Styles

Just as we saw in the preceding period, counter-hooliganism policing policies continued to be influenced during this period by the prevailing crime control model and the state of police cooperation in Europe. As a consequence, they were affected by both the spread of the risk-based social control model and the expansion of the policing of football hooliganism at the European level. In the former case, policies for countering the phenomenon, which were influenced by the risk management principle, increasingly involved the enforcement of proactive measures against football supporters which, in practice, entailed the introduction and/or more widespread use of many surveillance and control devices which were detrimental to civil liberties. In the case of the internationalization of policing, the homogenization of domestic policing policies under way during this period, which was influenced by the accelerated pace of Europeanization and the ensuing gradual convergence of justice and internal security policies at the national level, was particularly evident in the implementation of crowd control strategies at the national level and in the ongoing strengthening of cooperation at both the national and international levels. In addition to these two main influences, there was a third which grew out of the general changes that had occurred within the security realm, namely, the gradual privatization of crowd control within the stadia.

The policing of football hooliganism developed from the emerging regulatory framework which we examined earlier swiftly shed its earlier country-specific variations because, being still reliant on crowd control policies, it was influenced by the standardization process affecting these at the European level. Schematically speaking, it revolved around their three main axes (Della Porta 1995; Della Porta and Reiter 1998; Fillieule and Della Porta 2006), namely, restricting the use of violence as far as possible, tolerating minor offences in order to prevent the outbreak or escalation of football-related incidents, and prioritizing intelligence-gathering. The changes that had taken place in the policing of crowds thus signalled the future shape of preventive counter-hooliganism policies, the strengthening of which had been sought by the authors of the 1985 European Convention, as well as many other subsequent regulatory texts adopted by both European Community bodies and UEFA.

1 Policing and the perception of threat

The first two axes, which confirmed the validity of the policies followed in Northern European countries and led to the exclusively repressive policies used in Southern European countries being gradually replaced by preventive strategies,[1] prompted public security agents to plan and moderate their actions. Mirroring the actions of football hooligans whose activities, in response to the tightening of controls inside stadia, had undergone a temporal and spatial displacement, police strategies from then on made a similar shift in time and space to encompass both the pre- and post-match periods as well as any other places outside of stadia where incidents might occur. However, though they seemed viable, these policies soon showed their limitations. The fact that they had not been designed autonomously meant that they were linked so inextricably to the actions of the football hooligans that they led to a real 'battle of wits' (Williams et al. 1986: 584) which dragged all the actors involved into a descending spiral of violence with no way out. Since this type of approach, by definition, ruled out de-escalation, the way in which football hooliganism manifested itself from then on reflected the fact that each side was increasingly engaged in planning action strategies that would continue to reinforce each other *ad infinitum*. In other words, with no referents other than the forms in which the conflict manifested itself, policing of the phenomenon lost any innovatory impulse it may have had and consisted only of the outcome, however temporary, of the interaction between certain initiatives taken by each of the parties in conflict. Its intention was no longer to resolve but to eliminate or, at the very least, contain conflict by attacking only its obvious symptoms. Thus, far from yielding the expected results, it led to increasingly serious football-related incidents insofar as it contributed towards their spatial–temporal displacement and helped to radicalize the activities of football hooligans who, precisely because they were seeking to avoid police controls inside stadia, began to take action in city centres or elsewhere before, during and after matches, frequently resorting to the use of weapons,[2] thereby making the task of controlling them all the more onerous and difficult, if not impossible.

This escalation of football hooliganism was facilitated all the more by the fact that its policing was hardly ever founded on the principle of negotiation (Tsoukala 2001: 168ff). Indeed, although regular recourse to negotiation had been widely recognized as being a crucial element of crowd management in the preceding years (Docters van Leeuwen 1990; Waddington 1993; Della Porta and Reiter 1996, 1998), public security agents had habitually refused to use this approach in dealing with football hooligans because the latter were not seen as social actors acting within the framework of any kind of institutional system and could therefore not be considered as potential interlocutors for the police (Della Porta 1998: 241–5). It is important to stress at this point that this approach, which prevailed in the UK, France and the countries of Southern Europe,[3] was also taken to varying degrees in countries[4] where softer methods of tackling football hooliganism, such as participation in socio-preventive programmes, were employed since it was possible for the two control policies to coexist as long as they operated at different times (outside of or on the day of matches) and/or because the way in which they encroached on each other varied from place to place. For example, while establishing contact with violent football supporters was an integral part of such preventive programmes, it did not usually form part of the counter-hooliganism policies used on match days.

In any event, the refusal to negotiate, whether absolute or relative, reflected in part the failure of the academic community to provide a socially and politically legitimate rational picture of football hooliganism and demonstrated, on the contrary, that, as a result of two distinct but interdependent processes, the phenomenon was seen as extremely threatening to the internal security of the countries concerned. As we have seen, the first of these processes consisted of stripping football hooliganism of any rational foundation by dissociating its actors from both their socio-economic context and the sporting milieu and by giving their behaviour an irrational, even pathological aura. This picture, which was very common among public and sporting authorities, nevertheless coexisted with one that was its diametrical opposite. In the latter, football hooligans were depicted as being very dangerous because they were extremely well organized (Armstrong and Giulianotti 1998: 124–5) and took action solely because they enjoyed getting involved in fights. Once football hooliganism was seen as irrational or as being heavily orchestrated for gratuitous purposes, it became just one of the many threats to European security which, as shown earlier, were under construction at that time and, as such, went from being one of the types of behaviour likely to be subjected to soft social regulation to being one which could only be handled by control apparatuses that operated according to the principles of the risk-focused social control model.

2 Policing and risk management

It is thus hardly surprising that, from then on, the policing of football hooliganism increasingly turned to the third main axis of crowd control: intelligence-gathering. It was this that led to the widespread use of electronic surveillance inside and outside of stadia, the undercover policing of football supporters' groups in some countries[5] and the setting-up of information centres to identify football hooligans in the UK, the Netherlands and Germany. Although the establishment of these first information centres in countries with decentralized police systems arguably stemmed from the need for centralization and coordinated action rather than the conscious selection of a specific model of social control, it should be stressed that the importance accorded to remote control devices and the sorting and profiling inherent in the recording of data was consistent with the risk management principles.

Of course, early on, it was officials from the UK-based National Criminal Intelligence Service/Football Unit[6] who jumped at the opportunity opened up by the 1985 European Convention to institutionalize the control of deviance by compiling files on numerous known and potential troublemakers, distributing them widely to their foreign counterparts whenever an English club or the national team were involved in an international tournament, and finding as many sources as possible to feed into their database, which consisted of information supplied by both public and private security agents and anyone else deemed to be reliable. It was these same officials who were also criticized for arbitrarily collecting photos for inclusion in their database, artificially inflating the number of files[7] and tolerating abuses by certain undercover police officers who were acting as *agents provocateurs* – strategies which, in the eyes of their critics, sought to exaggerate the threat posed by football hooliganism in order to justify the introduction and further development of new surveillance devices (Armstrong and Hobbs 1994; Greenfield and Osborn 1996).

Even though their German and Dutch counterparts adhered more strictly to the law and thus avoided the abuses that took place in the UK in relation to data-gathering, they too were unable to steer entirely clear of the control of deviance or to guarantee optimum transparency with regard to data conservation, transfer and access. For example, in the Netherlands, judges who were ordered to rule on a matter relating to football hooliganism could, by special dispensation, have access to the database held by the Centraal Informatiepunt Voetbalvandalisme (CIV) in order to find out how many times the accused had been arrested in the past (Groenevelt 2002), thus making the sentence they imposed contingent on the supposedly dangerous character of the individual concerned.

In fact, as tools designed to meet the objectives of actuarial risk management, these surveillance devices could not help but reproduce the weaknesses and contradictions of the risk-focused social control model as far as protecting public and democratic order in the countries involved was concerned. The very setting up of such an apparatus showed that police action was determined by objectives that had been fixed in advance, pursuant to some kind of assessment of the dangerousness of a section of the population. The criteria employed to make such assessments were unclear, with members of at-risk groups being classified either according to their actual dangerousness, as confirmed by their entry into the criminal justice system, or their potential level of dangerousness which, though existing only in virtual space–time, had very real consequences – real, not only in the sense that being registered in a police database could result in an individual being subjected to other penalties, such as football bans, but also in that the use of surveillance devices inevitably ensured that punishable acts would be detected because the increased visibility of the individuals under surveillance left them at greater risk of being caught by security agents. Once detected, such criminality constituted *a posteriori* vindication of any initial suspicions, legitimized the existing security apparatus and bolstered calls for it to be further strengthened. Surveillance devices therefore became genuine political tools which, through their use in the game of defining sources of danger to security and ranking the values to be protected, could serve to legitimize security policies (Hörnqvist 2004: 40), justify attacks on civil liberties and the rule of law, precisely because they were protecting society against the security threat in question, and support the security services involved in calling for an increase in human and material resources so that they could carry on and even improve the work being done to tackle the supposed sources of disorder.

Justified on the grounds of the alleged dangerousness of football hooliganism, this control of deviance did not elicit any particular reactions on the part of the civil societies involved or even on the part of EC bodies. Thus, the European Parliament, in its Resolution of 21 May 1996 on hooliganism and the free movement of football supporters, denounced the fact that the existing filing system and exchange of data had 'resulted in the detention or expulsion of innocent persons' (European Parliament 1996c: 10), but nevertheless accepted measures to restrict the free movement, even of potential troublemakers, if they 'pose[d] a genuine and serious threat to public safety' (European Parliament 1996c: 26). Not wishing, however, to endorse the widespread control of deviance that would ensue, it specified that it would like to see the Council draw up a definition of the concept of the high-risk fan and lay down clear rules for the setting up, gathering, treatment and exchange of information (European Parliament 1996c: 50). However, no specific action has been taken so far to comply with its request.

3 The rise and growth of multilateral cooperation

Once data are collected, they are assessed within the framework of the police cooperation network set up at that time, and which has continued to grow at both the national and international levels ever since. Indissociable from the ongoing process of Europeanization, this enhancement of cooperation in the context of combating football hooliganism also reflected the growing importance of the spread of the global threat perception (Bigo 1996), which from then on prompted national security agencies to work together more closely and open up channels of communication with their foreign counterparts in order to confront as best they could what they saw as a continuum of transnational and interconnected threats to the security of European countries.

The existence of a common interest, namely, that of improving methods of fighting crime, and the *de facto* convergence around these deterritorialized threats thus began to bring together many different security services: police working on serious international crime, police working on forms of crime which, though less serious, were deemed to constitute a threat to security, the intelligence services and even military personnel working on non-military or transnational threats (Anderson and den Boer 1994; Marenin 1995; Anderson et al. 1996). As a consequence, during this period, in the case of many matters they were trying to resolve, agents from these various security services became dependent on data sent from abroad, data-processing systems, such as the Schengen Information System (SIS) or the Interpol databases, and the liaison officers who coordinated contact between the different police forces within Europe (Bigo 1999: 131–2). Though it is not easy to draw clear dividing lines between these parallel processes, they appear to be mutually reinforcing at the conceptual level, with Europeanization, in addition, enabling the technical aspects of this (inter)national cooperation between security agencies to be regulated. In other words, this rapprochement stemmed from the adoption of a series of new concepts, through which the security threat and the strategies and methods for combating it had been redefined, as well as the desire to speed up the pace of European integration[8] by, among other things, standardizing policies for protecting internal security. However, at the same time, the implementation of policing policies for meeting these new imperatives was greatly facilitated by Europeanization, which provided the legal framework and technical tools that made it possible for them to be enforced throughout Europe.

In the case of football hooliganism, while police cooperation grew as a result of the two processes referred to above, this was an approach that had also been prioritized in the counter-hooliganism policy advocated by the authors of the 1985 European Convention and, shortly afterwards, UEFA officials. The Council of Europe and UEFA did not only have an influence in terms of quantity, to the extent that they acted in addition to the other two processes; they also changed the very nature of cooperation. Given that the type of cooperation they wanted went beyond the bounds of mere police cooperation, over the years two types of cooperation emerged, one at the national level, the other at the international level.

At the national level, cooperation expanded to include all actors involved – local politicians, football club officials and, in some countries, private security agents. Increasingly regular consultation involving all actors took place in a growing number of countries with regard to the day-to-day management of football hooliganism and was obligatory in all countries whenever a high-risk match was to be played. Within the context of this broader cooperation, public security agents naturally played a pivotal role, though at the same time their power was checked precisely because they were obliged to work jointly with other actors. To be more specific, profiting from their status as experts, they had a key role in defining the threat and the strategies to be adopted. This position of superiority was further underpinned by their technical know-how and the specific knowledge they had thanks to the data collected by their colleagues, as well as by the implicit support they received because of the spread of this pattern of domination throughout the country. These 'operators of domination' (Foucault 1997: 39) thus depended on each other and sought to impose their view of things by basing the legitimacy of their power on their knowledge and supposed ability to speak the truth precisely because of the specific knowledge they alone possessed (Foucault 1997: 159ff).

Although this position of domination did indeed lead to the adoption of increasingly uniform strategies at the national level, it did not necessarily have the same consequences because public security agents were often forced to give in to the specific political and economic stakes and interests of their partners. Thus, in the UK, alcohol bans in a sporting context were gradually relaxed as a result of pressure from the management of sports clubs,[9] and in Greece, several measures provided in law were only belatedly and/or partially enforced due to a lack of collaboration from sporting bodies,[10] while the privatization of security inside stadia has, for several years now, been the subject of fierce negotiations that reflect differing political and economic interests (Mastrogiannakis 2008).

Conflicts and power struggles, albeit of a different nature, also took place between the different public security agencies called on to cooperate to implement the new counter-hooliganism policy. These differences, which were the result of the often strained relationship between civilian and military police forces, different local traditions with regard to policing strategies and practices, especially in countries with a decentralized police system, and different perceptions of the dangerousness of the phenomenon and/or the task of the security agents responsible for its control (O'Neill 2006), were damaging to the effective enforcement of legislative measures and even policing strategies at the national level.[11] From this point of view, the enhancement of police cooperation did lead to improved coordination of the measures to be taken and a certain standardization of strategies, in that it put a stop to the quasi-autonomous functioning of various police forces by introducing consultation at every level of decision-making, thereby creating quasi-obligatory channels of communication between the different security agencies involved.

At the international level, cooperation developed mainly between public security agencies, with the other actors getting involved only at the stage of implementing strategies that had been established by the former. This international cooperation, which was closely tied in with the international football tournament schedule, was first introduced for the 1988 European Championship, began to be stepped up at the time of the 1990 World Cup, and only became routine during the 1996 European Championship when, for the first time, a coordination centre was set up to enable the police forces from all the countries participating in the tournament to share information. The implementation of international cooperation, which led to the holding of numerous meetings, usually in the host country well before the match or tournament in question was due to take place, relied on an expanding network of liaison officers and spotters and gave paramount importance to the gathering and sharing of intelligence.

The first countries to have intelligence units specifically devoted to football hooliganism thus found themselves best placed because, by requiring other European countries to create posts and adopt practices that were similar to their own, their agents were able to impose *de facto* their own pattern of policing. In this quest for power, which relied on dissemination of a national model of social control, together with its underlying definition of the phenomenon to be controlled, it was the British security agents who, by setting up their own method of managing football hooliganism as the model for all the other European countries to follow, quickly achieved hegemony. By pointing to the experience their services had in dealing with the phenomenon due to its longstanding presence in their country and the fact that they had pioneered many of the measures taken to combat it, they managed to erase the image of failure from which their previous policy suffered[12] and present themselves as the undisputed experts on the subject within Europe.

This promotion of a policing model, which at the same time guaranteed the ideological promotion of the risk-based crime control policy, gave rise to major misgivings abroad precisely because it sought to apply the guiding principles of a highly controversial social control model. The creation of liaison officer posts, the establishment of files, the definition of the content of such files and the data that could be sent abroad, the way in which such files were compiled – all these points sowed discord between the different national security agencies who, to varying degrees, objected to this move towards the British reference model. However, since the British model was fully consistent with the new risk management policies, its promotion indirectly benefited from the increasing influence of its ideological reference model so that any reluctance on the part of certain national security agencies to go down that route[13] ended up being seen as evidence of laxity and/or a lack of administrative organization rather than a sign of fundamental disagreement.

Even though the development of cooperation at the international level had had to overcome the disagreements already mentioned and its development at the national level had come up against various types of conflicts and power struggles, the transfer of policing practices and know-how that it involved did not encounter any particular obstacles. In fact, from then on, football hooliganism started to become a domain into which measures already in use for combating other types of crime could be imported. At the international level, the creation of a network of liaison officers was thus inspired by similar networks set up in the 1970s in the context of combating drug trafficking and went on being developed at the instigation of the TREVI group (Massé 1992: 805). At the national level, the UK was the first to tackle football hooliganism by using measures that had up to then been mainly employed in combating terrorism and certain types of serious urban violence. Such measures included the undercover policing of football supporters' groups, a tactic which, prior to that, had been used in the context of combating the IRA, as well as during the 1981 urban riots and the 1984 miners' strike (Cappelle 1989: 62; Armstrong and Hobbs 1994: 199), and the setting up of a telephone line for receiving information about possible incidents and those responsible for them which, prior to that, had been used in countering terrorism.

Also closely tied in with this expansion of cooperation at both the national and international levels was the involvement of the private sector in the management of football hooliganism. Widely implemented in the second half of the 1980s, first in the UK and shortly afterwards in the Netherlands and other European countries, the privatization of the control of football supporters inside stadia was, in fact, consistent with the changes taking place in the field of security management as a whole (Nogala 1996) which, following the emergence of risk management, saw the development of security networks within both the public and private domains. The splintering of sources of insecurity arising from the endless proliferation of threats and risks was accompanied by a burgeoning of security management, with public security agencies seeking partnerships with private actors whom they saw as co-providers of public security (Bayley and Shearing1996; Ericson and Haggerty 1997; Loader 2000). From then on, in this vast web of security management, the actions of public bodies became just one of several possible sources of control, order and authority within society, alongside those of private actors and even members of civil society (Loader 2000: 328; Johnston and Shearing 2003: 145ff; Dorn and Levi 2007).

In the case of football hooliganism, the privatization of control of football supporters inside stadia, which stemmed from the wish for security production to be shared, was expressed, above all, in a call for joint responsibility for controlling events which, *in fine*, were merely a very lucrative form of leisure.[14] It needs to be stressed, nevertheless, that this call for shared responsibility was underpinned by a series of corporatist demands. First, public security agencies were seeking to cut the ever-increasing costs of controlling stadia, which were not being satisfactorily covered by football club managements. By cooperating with the private sector, they could also significantly cut back on the number of staff devoted to this task, the successful accomplishment of which, especially in the case of high-risk matches, required the mass mobilization of forces on the ground and even the bringing in of reinforcements, thereby disrupting the smooth operation of other police work and diverting resources from the task of safeguarding people and property in other parts of the area in question. Lastly, allocating the control of football supporters inside stadia to the private sector allowed public security agencies to improve their image to the extent that they were no longer the only ones facing criticism for the ineffectiveness of their management of the phenomenon both in specific cases[15] and in the long term.

The gradual expansion throughout this period of the privatization of control of football supporters inside stadia in many European countries did not, however, succeed in overcoming certain obstacles that stemmed mainly from the degree to which football supporters were organized. It was therefore easy for privatization to be applied in countries where, in the absence of large organized football supporters' groups, it was possible to hand over total responsibility to private security agents for searching football supporters on entering stadia, directing the public within stadia and calming tensions and possible conflicts before, where necessary, calling in police reinforcements.[16] However, it was hard to impose in countries where the level of organization of football supporters' groups was such that it was feared private security agents would be unable to effectively keep control of them.[17]

Despite these limitations, its implementation in the management of football hooliganism meant that from then on the private sector became one of the primary actors within that sphere. It should be underlined, nevertheless, that the growing importance of the place accorded to the private sector did not in any way mean that the role of the public sector was substantially weakened. In fact, the increasing power of the private sector was largely counterbalanced by, on the one hand, the introduction of electronic surveillance within stadia and, on the other, the stronger role played by public agencies in gathering and managing information and coordinating policy. In other words, public security agents remained masters of the situation by retaining for themselves overall supervision of operations, thanks to the use of remote control devices (Rose and Miller 1992), the implementation and management of which were subcontracted to private actors. Within this division of labour, the state, by retaining its monopoly on the use of violence, remained the main security provider while private actors were responsible for establishing security networks based on the principles of actuarial risk management (Osborne and Gaebler 1993; Shearing 2001: 212–13).

4 Long-term prevention policies

In this context in which both the causes of insecurity and the number of actors involved in the production of security were proliferating, some countries sought to develop alternative strategies for managing football hooliganism with a view to establishing a long-term prevention policy. First seen in Germany in 1981, under the name of *Fan Projekts*, this policy, which spread from the mid-1980s onwards, reaching the Netherlands in 1986, Belgium in 1988 and other European countries later on, was not promoted by the European Community and Council of Europe until the following period (Council of Europe 1999b, 2003a; European Commission 2007).

Breaking with the actuarial risk management model, this policy, which continued to take inspiration from the principles of the rehabilitation-oriented crime control model, consisted of establishing long-term collaboration between football supporters and public security agents, with social workers acting as mediators, and between supporters and their football clubs. Based on the implicit acceptance of the social roots of football hooliganism and always organized around a single football club, the actors involved in the German *Fan Projekts* sought to distance football supporters from violence by intervening not only on match days but also during the rest of the week. On match days, they acted as mediators between the football supporters and the public and/or private security agents in order to defuse tensions and establish a channel of communication between young people and the social control agents. During the rest of the week, they took on a long-term educational and social role by gaining the trust of the football supporters, systematically accompanying them to places they frequented in their ordinary lives, supporting them with administrative matters,[18] suggesting sporting and cultural activities, obtaining professional advice for them,[19] helping them to organize their football supporter activities better,[20] and so on. Over the years, these projects, which were funded by the football clubs,[21] grew in number to cover several divisions in a number of regions of the country and began to yield fruit in the sense that they managed to disrupt the generational renewal of football hooligans.

Influenced by the German model, the Netherlands and Belgium imported this strategy (Esman and Adang 2005) and adapted it to their own national or even local specificities but without betraying its guiding principles. The only project that was significantly different was the Belgian one, known as *Fan Coaching*, which was funded solely by the government, thus enabling them to adopt, where necessary, a critical position vis-à-vis football clubs or the Belgian Football Federation (Comeron 1992, 2002; Comeron and Vanbellingen 2002). Designed and long supported by Belgian academics,[22] in collaboration with sporting bodies and the cities concerned, *Fan Coaching* was welcomed by both security professionals and football supporters and, even if these days it is used more by Walloon football clubs than Flemish ones, it is invariably cited as being one of the reasons for the reduction in football hooliganism both inside and outside the country.[23]

In fact, the main contribution *Fan Coaching* made to counter-hooliganism policies was that it changed attitudes in two ways. First, it inculcated young football supporters with respect for rules and representatives of the authorities while downgrading the image of the violent hooligan; and second, it influenced the way all the actors involved in controlling young people perceived them. By deliberately taking an integrated approach, this primary prevention policy extended the network of multilateral cooperation by setting up many different arenas in which dialogue and information exchange could take place.[24] The channels of communication thus established between public security agencies, social workers and academics gradually brought about a change in attitudes and the ideas that were being passed from one to another, with security professionals having to agree to learn from the theoretical and empirical knowledge of social workers and academics who, in turn, had to acquaint themselves with organizational constraints and policing priorities. Consolidated by means of extensive research funded by the Belgian police, this dialogue allowed a better understanding of the world of the football supporter and the problems raised by the policing of it to be attained and shared, and improved the quest for optimum solutions. Since this multifaceted influence, by definition, relativized the importance of the place attributed to policing strategies based on the actuarial risk management model, public security agents did not appear to move away from that route until the ensuing period when faced with the prospect of organizing Euro 2000.

At the same time, it should be pointed out that this expansion of cooperation seems to have had considerable, but not necessarily similar, consequences for the actors involved. Indeed, while the establishment of these channels between social workers and security agents allowed the latter to become aware of the social origins of the phenomenon and, by extension, to recognize the usefulness of undertaking educational work to calm down potentially violent football supporters, it also invited social workers to refrain from criticizing law enforcement agencies and, consequently, to recognize the usefulness of the work done by the police in managing football hooliganism (Comeron 2002: 26–7). Their mediation work was thus bound to be moderate in character, thereby either stripping them of their ability to openly defend the rights of football supporters or immediately neutralizing any criticisms they might have of the validity of the control and surveillance measures used in dealing with football hooliganism. So, despite efforts to label all mediation initiatives as 'offensive prevention', in order to show that the target group was not seen only as a source of risk against which it was necessary to protect oneself by restricting the freedoms of its members but also as a source of positive possibilities that it was worth helping to develop (Kellens 1997: 121), the creation of national information centres across Europe, for example, was not presented as part of an apparatus that would expand the control of deviance and possibly infringe the civil liberties of football supporters, but as a necessary measure for improving prevention of the phenomenon (Comeron 2002: 51).

8
The General Acceptance of 'Otherness'

Although football hooliganism's transformation into a serious public order problem was the result of many factors, the media coverage given to it, as has been pointed out, seems to have been mainly determined by the impact of the Heysel tragedy across Europe. Unfairly attributed solely to English football hooligans,[1] this event, which received huge media coverage, in a way confirmed the image of football hooligans as 'monsters' and justified the implementation of whatever measures might be deemed appropriate to take against them. My own analysis of the British, French and Greek quality press,[2] together with existing studies of the Italian press, shows clearly that, from then on, social construction of 'otherness' was consolidated in those places where it had already been apparent, namely in the UK, and introduced permanently into countries where it had been weak or even nonexistent. Thus, while the Greek press still resembled the Italian press of the 1970s, the French and Italian press began to represent the issue by using discursive methods hitherto employed mainly in the UK. Although this tendency had been evident in Italy since the early 1980s, it only began to appear in France in 1993 after extensive media coverage was given to an attack on members of special police units at the Paris Saint-Germain stadium.

The growth in the spread of the social construction of 'otherness' was not only quantitative, it was also qualitative. All the main methods by which this had been done during the preceding period were now reinforced, not only because they were employed more often, and in more countries, but also because they became commonplace in the press and were increasingly frequently used even by representatives of the authorities. The political affiliation of the newspapers studied does not seem to have significantly influenced whether or not this approach was taken – which indicates that general acceptance of the social 'otherness' and dangerousness of football hooligans existed over and above the usual political divisions. Furthermore, the adoption of this approach does not seem to have been influenced by the specific ways in which football hooliganism manifested itself in the countries concerned. Thus, since French, Italian and Greek football hooligans were hardly ever involved in incidents abroad, these ways of representing the issue were adopted mainly with regard to its manifestation at home. On the other hand, in the UK, after the initial reaction to the Heysel tragedy had died down, football hooliganism gradually disappeared from the press as a domestic issue, only to reappear whenever incidents broke out abroad. Reflecting in part the gradual restoration of calm to stadia in the then First Division and in part a concern to minimize the problem in order to speed up the return of English football clubs to European competition, the position of the press seems well summed up in the following statement: 'Soccer hooligans are has-beens, as dead as a pop group who haven't had a hit for five years. Until they go abroad' (*The Times*, 16 June 1992: 14).

1 Football hooliganism in the British press

The British broadsheets of course continued to avoid using the war-like rhetoric so beloved of the tabloids but, following the example of the prime minister who, the day after Heysel, called football hooligans 'thugs' (*The Times*, 31 May 1985: 1) and a sports minister who, five years later, called them 'louts' (*Guardian*, 11 July 1990),[3] they no longer hesitated to label them 'thugs' and 'yobs', even in main headlines (*The Times*, 21 June 1988: 14). Spreading disorder within whichever country they were visiting, once they were abroad football hooligans, who were a real 'disgrace to civilized society' (*The Times*, 15 June 1988: 10),[4] regularly sullied the country's international reputation (*Guardian*, 16 June 1992: 6),[5] thereby making their compatriots feel ashamed of them (*The Times*, 15 June 1988: 10).

The spread of this anti-social image of football hooligans was reinforced by one of irrationality which, from then on, predominated. Following on from the key patterns of representation employed during the previous period, football hooligans were often portrayed as being mentally deficient or irresponsible because they were under the influence of alcohol. They could therefore be called 'stupid' (*The Times*, 21 June 1988: 14), a 'moronic minority' (*Independent*, 17 June 1992: 32) or 'drunken Neanderthals' (*The Times*, 16 June 1992: 14). Not confined solely to journalistic discourse, this form of representation could be found in the political domain. Thus, while a sports minister saw them as a 'mindless minority' (*Independent*, 18 June 1990: 2), a Conservative MP described them as 'empty-headed' (*Guardian*, 16 June 1992: 6). The image of irrationality which predominated from then on was also taken up by police representatives. It was therefore hardly surprising when, in 1996, at a symposium organized by the French Interior Ministry in connection with the hosting of the 1998 World Cup, all the British police and intelligence officers who spoke invariably described English football hooligans as 'idiots' when addressing their French counterparts.[6] This institutionalization of the dissociation of football hooligans from the rest of society also applied to their links with the sporting world. The idea that they were not genuine supporters and were only 'vaguely interested in football' (*Independent*, 21 June 1992: 8), which was widespread in the press, was thus taken up by a sports minister, who made a clear distinction between the 'criminally motivated minority of so-called England fans' (*Guardian*, 28 June 1990)[7] and 'the real fans' (*Independent*, 4 July 1990: 16).

Just as in the previous period, this severing of football hooligans from the rest of the community was accompanied by the increasing prevalence of an approach that failed to make any in-depth analysis of their behaviour.[8] When not considered to be the 'anarchic and pointless' (*The Times*, 16 June 1992: 14), even 'gratuitous' (*Guardian*, 18 June 1992: 21), behaviour of people 'who just want to fight' (*The Times*, 21 June 1988: 14),[9] this type of violence provoked an extremely limited causal discourse which refused to give any consideration to the social profile of football supporters. So the social origins of football hooliganism remained either vague, 'ranging from Original Sin to Andy Warhol's "15 minutes of fame"' (*Independent*, 21 June 1992: 22), or were only clearly identifiable as symptoms of various 'social evils'. In the case of the latter, they revealed 'a disease of a prosperous society [caused by] young people with more money than the previous generation' (*Guardian*, 1 June 1985: 1)[10] or were related to a decline in values, reflecting the 'moral vacuum into which working class life has descended' (*The Times*, 16 June 1992: 14) or the inability of young people 'to achieve self-control or order for lack of an internalised model' (*Guardian*, 18 June 1992: 20). The social origins of the phenomenon were also linked to alcohol consumption, with one Conservative MP describing football hooligans as 'beer-bellied louts' (*Guardian*, 16 June 1992: 6), as well as nationalism and xenophobia (*Independent*, 17 June 1988: 15, 18 June 1990: 18; *Guardian*, 18 June 1992: 21) and the influence of extreme right-wing values (*Independent*, 11 June 1990: 2, 21 June 1992: 22). The circle of responsibility was only broadened to incorporate the media who, on the one hand, were 'elaborating urban myths which are irresistibly seductive to the impressionable; sporadic thuggery is turned into an icon of class identification' and, on the other, inciting violence since, 'under the guise of condemnation, they [the tabloids] in fact serve as the most prized arena for notoriety within the delinquent community' (*The Times*, 16 June 1992: 14).

Whether excluded from the world of sensible individuals because of their above-mentioned mental deficiencies, from the world of law-abiding citizens because of their criminal nature, from the world of true supporters because of their rejection of fair play and their tendency to resort to violence, and even from the civilized world as a whole because of their barbaric behaviour, football hooligans had been severed from all the familiar frames and repertoires of collective action which are acceptable within our societies. They were therefore seen as particularly threatening precisely because they had been divorced from all the points of reference normally used to make any kind of collective action understandable.

Having been reduced simply to constituting the embodiment of certain 'social evils', they were, quite naturally, seen as the manifestation of a pathological state. From then on so commonplace that it was taken up even by academics (Williams 1988), the use of medical terms such as 'sickness' and 'disease' to describe their behaviour often became even more specific. Football hooliganism which, the day after the Heysel tragedy, had been compared to a 'contagious virus' (*Guardian*, 31 May 1985: 14) was regularly referred to as a 'scourge' (*Independent*, 16 February 1995: 40) and sometimes compared to the 'plague' (*The Times*, 15 June 1988: 48; *Guardian*, 18 June 1992: 20). Like such epidemics which used to spread uncontrollably throughout Europe and ravage populations, the threat it posed now hung heavily over the well-being of the communities concerned and could be removed only by implementing very strict controls, inevitably including the placing of those who may be contaminated into quarantine.

Once it had been defined in this way, the threat which this phenomenon represented for society was amplified by means of self-fulfilling prophecies. Pushing journalists' normal forecasting abilities to the extreme (Neveu 2001/2004: 52), these were constructed well in advance of the sporting events in question on the basis of assumptions derived from past incidents, analyses made by police and/or intelligence officers, fears expressed by local politicians and/or sports officials and, where relevant, statements made by certain football supporters. The more risky the future fixture was seen to be, the more numerous, extensive and detailed such self-fulfilling prophecies were and the tenser the atmosphere on the day of the match became. In the event that incidents actually took place, they were presented as foreseeable, if not long predicted, thus confirming the existence of an ongoing and hence extremely worrying climate of disorder. The absence of incidents, on the other hand, was never interpreted as a sign that the situation had been wrongly assessed, but as evidence that the event had been effectively policed. Already in existence in the preceding period, this fear-fuelling coverage of football hooliganism now assumed significant proportions, especially at the time of international tournaments. A turning point occurred at the time of the 1988 European Championship when the tabloids started to compile lists of the most dangerous football hooligans (Williams et al. 1984/1989: LI) and the quality press labelled the tournament the 'International Hooligan Championships' (*The Observer*, 19 June 1988: 15). The expectation that violence would occur, as demonstrated by such over-the-top tabloid headlines as 'World War III' (*Sun*, 13 June 1988),[11] was even evident in articles written by academics (Williams 1988).

In the absence of serious incidents,[12] the conventional image of the dangerousness of football hooliganism was fuelled by suggesting the possibility of future incidents, with the threat being shifted from one event to another, depending on the level of 'dangerousness' of the football supporters concerned (*The Times*, 15 June 1990: 48). The ways in which journalists presented the phenomenon took on all the more weight because they were later backed up by numerous statements from police representatives. Using the data collected by their intelligence services, the latter were able to announce, for example, prior to the start of the 1990 World Cup, that '[w]e have got a lot of good intelligence about plans being made that will involve the Dutch – plans for hooligan activity' (*Independent*, 31 May 1990: 3).[13]

Far from being an isolated form of intervention, statements of this kind showed the increasingly important position the police occupied from then on in media coverage of the phenomenon. This was illustrated by the first lengthy journalistic descriptions of the security apparatus (*Guardian*, 8 June 1992: 9) and by calls from police representatives for more stringent legislation (*Guardian*, 18 June 1992: 22). It was also demonstrated indirectly by the virtual absence of any criticism of the existing control apparatus or of the demands for it to be strengthened.[14] The ever-increasing appeals for the counter-hooliganism control apparatus to be enhanced became particularly insistent at the time of international tournaments. In 1988, for example, the measures so far introduced were described as being 'minor cosmetic adjustments', undertaken by a government 'which has so far shown itself incapable, or unwilling, to tackle the crisis head on'. The UK was further said to resemble a 'zoo of dangerous animals' that harmed 'the credibility of British society' (*The Times*, 15 June 1988: 48).

Widely used in Europe in the immediate aftermath of the Heysel tragedy (*The Times*, 31 May 1985: 4), this animal imagery, occasionally reinforced by images of barbarism and savagery (*Guardian*, 30 May 1985: 1; *Independent*, 14 June 1992: 4), from then on became so common that it was even taken up by foreign police representatives (*Guardian*, 8 June 1992: 9, 18 June 1992: 20).[15] Yet, as observed elsewhere with regard to other social groups,[16] this reducing of members of a social group to the level of animals is in fact a crucial stage of a process whereby they are deprived of the right to have rights – these, by definition, being reserved for human beings (Burgat 1999: 45). So if the image of football hooligans as irrational can justify the quasi-exclusive adoption of security measures, their animalization can even justify the adoption of measures that are detrimental to civil liberties.

2 Football hooliganism in the Italian and French press

During this period, the image of the 'football hooligan threatening the well-being of the community' began to feature prominently in the Italian and French press. In Italy, while the turning point was clearly illustrated by a statement the Minister of Public Works made the day after Heysel, in which he called English football hooligans 'drunken barbarians' (*The Times*, 31 May 1985: 4), the use of terms stigmatizing such violence also started to become commonplace in relation to Italian football hooligans. As a result of the same discursive construction of 'otherness' as witnessed in the British press, the latter became increasingly cut off from the rest of society by being, for example, regularly presented as 'idiots' and 'beasts' (Dal Lago 1992) or 'new barbarians' (*La Repubblica*, 31 January 1995: 7).[17] The powerful rise of the image of the young 'rebel without a cause' (Marchi 2005: 101) gradually established the idea that such violence was gratuitous by marginalizing any causal analysis of this behaviour (Dal Lago and Moscati 1992; Louis 2008: 134–9). During the 1990s, with fear also being regularly fuelled by self-fulfilling prophecies, football hooliganism was so often described as an expression of social pathology comparable to 'cancer' (*La Repubblica*, 31 January 1995: 7) that urgent calls for the existing legislation to be strictly enforced and for the security apparatus to be enhanced became increasingly common in both the conservative and liberal press (Louis 2008: 136; Marchi 2005).

At the same time, this image of anomie surrounding the conduct of football supporters, which was backed up by the extensive use of metaphors in which, for example, the stadium was described as the 'Far West of football's unpunished' (*La Repubblica*, 12 February 1995: 2), was coupled with a different type of analysis, linking the perpetuation of such violence with the very functioning of the sports field by openly alleging that there was collusion between football supporters and club officials (*La Repubblica*, 31 January 1995: 2, 4).

During this period, in France too the moderate coverage of the past gave way to patterns of representation of football hooliganism which tended to reproduce the image of the socially alien football hooligan. This new framework for presenting the phenomenon, which emerged only gradually, was initially reserved solely for foreign football supporters. Thus, the 'savage hordes' who, according to journalists, were going to invade Italy at the time of the 1990 World Cup (*Le Figaro*, 9–10 June 1990: 8) were, in the eyes of one scholar, made up of 'stupid' individuals who revealed the 'necrosis of society' (Raspaud 1990). From 1993, following intense media coverage of the incidents referred to above, this way of representing the issue also began to be used in connection with French football hooligans.

The turning point became evident with the increasingly frequent use of terms that stigmatized the anti-social behaviour of football hooligans, now called 'thugs' (*Le Figaro*, 31 August 1993: B-7) and 'yobs' (*Le Monde*, 8 June 1996: 20). Taken up also by the representatives of sporting authorities (*Le Monde*, 31 August 1993: 10), this stigmatization was for the first time accompanied by suggestions that such violence might be irrational and pathological. Football hooligans were thus described as 'cretins' (*Journal du Dimanche*, 29 August 1993: 11) and 'crazy fanatics' (*Le Figaro*, 31 August 1993: B-7), and football hooliganism was compared to a 'scourge' (*Le Monde*, 8 June 1996: 20).

The fear engendered by such abnormal behaviour was further fuelled by a process of criminalization which defined the dangerousness of football hooliganism not so much by how it was manifested in France, where it was still relatively rare, but by making analogies between it and other much more serious criminal phenomena. Thus, football supporters' groups were described as 'organized gangs' (*Le Figaro*, 31 August 1993: B-7) and one scholar had no hesitation in referring to them as 'armed gangs who impose a reign of terror wherever they go' (J. M. Brohm, in *Journal du Dimanche*, 12 February 1995: 8). Since this fuelling of fear could not be justified by the scale of the phenomenon in France, incidents of violence that occurred there were examined from the European perspective. Detailed descriptions of the ways in which English or German football hooligans behaved and comparisons between French football hooligans and English 'casuals' thus helped to disseminate the idea that it was only a question of time before the phenomenon would strike France head-on, if it had not already happened (*Le Figaro*, 31 August 1993: B-7; *Journal du Dimanche*, 5 September 1993: 3).

Given this imminent threat, there were increasing calls for the counter-hooliganism control apparatus to be strengthened as a matter of urgency. It was thus believed that, since France was lagging behind other countries in combating football hooliganism, the most effective strategy would be to copy the Belgians, by having judges present at football stadia (*Le Figaro*, 31 August 1993: B-7), and the English and Germans, by turning to undercover policing, the widespread installation of CCTV cameras in stadia and intelligence-gathering (*Le Monde*, 31 August 1993: 10, 16 March 1996: 24). Following this same reasoning, football banning orders were presented as being particularly effective penalties because the absence up to then of any immediate visible punishment supposedly created a feeling of impunity among football supporters which encouraged the use of violence (*Journal du Dimanche*, 5 September 1993: 3). The importance accorded from then on to safeguarding security was also apparent in ever-longer descriptions of the security apparatuses adopted abroad during international tournaments (*Le Monde*, 8 June 1996: 20) or at high-risk matches in France (*Le Monde*, 16 March 1996: 24), as well as in the virtual absence of any criticism of such measures.

3 Football hooliganism in the Greek press

These ways of representing the issue stood in stark contrast to those adopted during most of this period by the Greek press which, by steering clear of stigmatizing football supporters who were usually simply called 'fanatics', looked in depth at the causes of their behaviour. More often than not, journalists preferred to leave the analysis to scholars. Thus, they often cited the first academic study carried out, which revealed that these young men, who often came from broken homes and were living in unstable socio-economic conditions, reflected the crisis in values taking place in a society that was becoming increasingly indifferent to a section of its young people because it was blighted by alienation, commercialization and amorality (*Vima*, 9 October 1988: 39–42; *Eleftherotypia*, 19 March 1990: 23–5; *Kathimerini*, 19 January 1992: 13). Having been defined in this way, the social profile of football hooligans was supplemented by representatives of football supporters' groups and even the football hooligans themselves, who were often asked for their views (*Nea*, 22 January 1986: 20–1; *Eleftherotypia*, 10 February 1992: 27–9). Their behaviour, which could not be dissociated from the way their society functioned, thus remained clearly circumscribed within a rational action framework. In this regard, it should be pointed out that, since Greek football hooligans tended to take drugs rather than drink alcohol, drug use was, of course, frequently mentioned (*Kathimerini*, 19 January 1992: 13), but as a specific cultural trait of a section of youth rather than as a factor that precipitated engagement in violence.

This causal approach also led journalists to broaden the circle of those responsible for football hooliganism so that it was attributed mainly to the questionable conduct of certain club officials who were accused of using the supporters of their clubs for their own advantage and of benefiting from the indulgence of the public authorities, who were sometimes reluctant even to enforce the law (*Vima*, 2 November 1986: 42; *Nea*, 17 February 1988: 16–17; *Eleftherotypia*, 19 March 1990: 23–5, 10 February 1992: 27–9). Responsibility was also attributed to political parties, who were loath to give football supporters a rough ride because they saw them as a not insignificant part of their electoral base (*Vima*, 17 February 1991: A43), and to the press, especially the sports press, who deliberately stirred up disputes between football supporters (*Nea*, 17 February 1988: 16–17).

Consequently, calls for the adoption of a new counter-hooliganism policy did not centre on the introduction of coercive measures but on the need to clean up professional football and apply the law effectively to all actors in the sporting field (*Eleftherotypia*, 19 March 1990: 23–5; *Vima*, 17 February 1991: A41). These calls were also accompanied by complaints about the absence of a long-term preventive policy that might allow the causes of the problem to be eradicated (*Kiriakatiki Eleftherotypia*, 2 November 1986: 25).

As we saw in the case of the Italian press during the 1970s, this kind of coverage did not reflect an absence of incidents. On the contrary, violence in Greek stadia had already led to the deaths of three football supporters, numerous injuries and significant material damage. In fact, this moderate coverage of football hooliganism reflected the unfinished social peace-building process that was taking place in a society which, having been racked by intense socio-political conflict ever since the fall of the military junta, did not feel particularly threatened by that specific type of youth violence. What is more, it felt even less threatened given that such violence was seen as either the result of the orchestration of football hooligans by club officials or the expression of a process of transition from adolescence to adulthood which might occasionally take the form of violent behaviour but never lasted (*Kiriakatiki Eleftherotypia*, 2 November 1986: 46). This perception of the phenomenon, which was broadly shared even by the police officers who were at that time in charge of addressing football hooliganism,[18] has also long accounted for their categorical rejection of any plan to establish a database of potential troublemakers.

This moderate coverage nevertheless began to change in the mid-1990s, gradually giving way to the forms of representation that increasingly prevailed in other countries. Reflecting Greek society's growing concern about rising crime, which was often attributed to foreigners (Tsoukala 2002), the mounting sense of insecurity in a country which up to then had been relatively shielded from crime was translated into, among other things, increasing intolerance of any type of disorder. Football hooliganism was thus presented as 'an important parameter of a particular type of criminality [which] is eroding the foundations of Greek society' and costs taxpayers vast amounts of money (*Vima*, 17 September 1995: A53). The image of disorder created by this kind of violence was from then on sustained by, among other things, the frequent use of statistics and lists of past incidents (*Vima*, 17 September 1995: A53; *Kathimerini*, 20–21 May 1995: 21). By the end of this period, football hooliganism was being described as 'pathological' (*Vima*, 2 February 1997: 29) and presented as something engaged in by 'people with problems' (*Kathimerini*, 23 February 1997).[19]

Part III
Splintered Contours (1997–2008)

Introduction to Part III

While I do not concur with Moorhouse who claimed that 'the debate on hooliganism has lost all power to generate any new social insights' (2000: 1464), it has to be said that, since the end of the twentieth century, the number of studies into the aetiology of football hooliganism has declined considerably. Apart from a few psychological theses, most of the theories developed during this period have tended to apply earlier models to countries where football hooliganism has become firmly entrenched, such as France, or countries where the social sciences are currently undergoing rapid development, such as Greece and Turkey.

As far as social control is concerned, the increasingly widespread use of apparatuses for proactively controlling risk behaviours, which were introduced during the preceding period, is now coupled with a proliferation of football hooliganism-related conceptual registers, resulting in greater legal vagueness. At the same time, the steady growth of the global threat perception and the constant strengthening of international police cooperation have meant that policing practices have often been transferred from one field of police activity to another, so that the phenomenon to be controlled has lost even more of its specificity. This splintering of the definitional profile of football hooliganism, which occurred first at the EU level and only later at national level, has endowed the social control apparatus with potentially infinite interventionist power, resulting in the institutionalization of the control and punishment of deviant groups. Currently, this interventionist power seems to be directed more towards the day-to-day management of football hooliganism, with the management of international tournaments being subjected to a broader range of policies which, while still consistent with the principles of actuarial risk management, are seeking to put the human factor back into crowd management.

The attention now paid to security and risk anticipation issues is also apparent in media representations of football hooliganism. The ever-present stereotypical image of the 'socially alien' and threatening football hooligan that adheres to the principles established during the preceding two periods is thus accompanied by an implicitly positive representation of security apparatuses and an enduring silence on the resulting breaches of football supporters' rights. In transcending countries and political divisions, such media coverage clearly shows that there is consensus around the need to protect at any price the internal security of European countries against any type of allegedly threatening behaviour. Having become an integral part of this process of constructing social threats and legitimizing security policies, journalists no longer act as a critical counterbalance to the increasingly tough social control apparatus and the dangers it poses to the rule of law and civil liberties.

9
The Academic Community Runs out of Steam

1 Psychological theses

In France, Olivier Le Noé (1998) now sees the thesis of ritualized violence and the search for social status as being one of the key explanations of the phenomenon and furthermore links outbreaks of violence to a series of circumstances, ranging from what is at stake in the match to the quality of the game and the political extremism of football supporters. The Turkish researchers Artun Ünsal (2004) and Kismet Erkiner (2004) have also taken a multifactorial approach, attributing football hooliganism to many different psychological parameters related to the architecture of stadia, poor refereeing and irresponsible behaviour on the part of football players, journalists and football club officials, as well as flawed policing.

In the UK, the thesis of ritualized violence, seen as a dominant form of behaviour that only shifts into real violence accidentally, has been taken up by Clifford Stott and his collaborators, who have focused on the role played in this respect by law enforcement agencies. Starting from the principle that football hooliganism can only be satisfactorily explained and controlled by taking account of the patterns of action and interactions between all the groups of actors involved, they have shown, through numerous field studies, that the way in which public security agents perceive football hooligans can give rise to inappropriate crowd control policies and thus trigger football-related incidents, just as in a self-fulfilling prophecy (Stott and Reicher 1998; Stott 2003; Stott et al. 2006, 2007; Stott and Pearson 2007).

These works do not suffer from the weaknesses mentioned earlier in connection with the ritualized violence thesis because they do not seek to minimize the extent of the actual violence and, further, they are based on solid empirical grounds. In seeking to respect the complexities of social reality, Stott has the merit of having broadened the circle of those responsible for football hooliganism to include public security agents, thus making it easier to comprehend the web of interactions that determine how this type of behaviour manifests itself. Nevertheless, this theory remains tentative because its conclusions are not contextualized. In other words, no account is taken of the political and bureaucratic interests and struggles that are likely to influence police perceptions, and consequently their handling, of behaviour that is threatening to internal security. Yet, these perceptions are the last link in a whole chain of interactions that take place within the political and security fields in any given country. Consequently, their effect on the development of football hooliganism cannot be properly assessed outside of the context from which they emerge and, where applicable, are supported, legitimized and disseminated.

2 Anthropological theses

The argument that actual violence in the behaviour of football supporters is rare has also been put in France by Nicolas Roumestan (1998) and in Greece by Dimitris Papageorgiou (1998), who, in their respective works, see fandom as a set of complex social rites of a highly carnivalesque nature which are mainly intended to assert masculine identity and give young men a stronger sense of belonging. In this context, violence has long tended to be sporadic and insignificant, occurring only when emotions have been stirred up in an atmosphere of inflamed antagonism and usually resulting from the uncontrolled excesses of a few individuals.

3 Sociological theses

3.1 Theories based on political sociology

While Taylor's thesis continues to influence researchers abroad, as evidenced by the work of the Italian academic Valerio Marchi (2005), in France Patrick Vassort (1999) has returned to Brohm's thesis. Pursuing the latter's line, he believes that football hooliganism simply reflects the internal logic of the functioning of football which, since it is determined by political or economic domination interests, inculcates in football supporters the cult of victory and leads them to get involved in segregationist and nationalist brawls.

3.2   Subcultural theses

The subcultural thesis has been taken up in France by Patrick Mignon, who sees football hooliganism as a type of masculine culture of violence (1998), and by Dominique Bodin who, based on a comparative study of football, basketball, rugby and volleyball spectators, refutes the idea that football hooliganism is due to a loss of cultural identity, linking it instead to the emergence of an age-based subculture focused on a search for identity. He further attributes its development to the adoption of anomic behaviour in stadia, stemming not only from a failure to enforce the law, but also from the social vacuum left by football club officials who have been too complacent about the excesses committed by supporters attending their matches (Bodin 1999, 2002; Bodin et al. 2004b).

Although the work of Bodin has the merit of addressing the issue of football hooliganism from a comparative perspective, his starting hypothesis that the phenomenon only exists in the footballing milieu (Bodin et al. 2004a, 2004b: 24) is contradicted by several studies showing that crowd disorder has also been observed at basketball, volleyball, ice hockey and water polo matches (Berger 1990; Busset 2002; Koukouris et al. 2004; Koukouris and Taxildaridis 2005). Furthermore, the part of it that deals with the aetiology of football hooliganism prompts two comments on its theoretical background. To be more specific, to the extent that these studies take up the thesis of an age-based subculture, it is only appropriate to reiterate the earlier criticisms made of that theory, namely, that it ignores other parameters that go to make up the social identity of football supporters as well as the role played by numerous non sports-related factors. On the other hand, to the extent that they make use of the Mertonian concept of anomie, they seem to be founded on a misinterpretation. According to Robert Merton (1957, 1964), anomie, as a factor explaining deviant behaviour, cannot be understood without considering certain characteristics of deviant individuals, such as their social origin, race or ethnicity. Yet Bodin disregards or minimizes the importance of these parameters and simply attributes the anomic behaviour of football supporters to a relaxation of social control. By so doing, rather than supporting the criticisms made by others concerning the vague and limited nature of Merton's theory (Lemert 1964: 60–1, 73–5; Short 1964: 100ff), he seems to be putting forward a kind of ideological argument around the relationship between order and disorder in society. This position has been further confirmed in his most recent works where, essentially taking up the neo-conservative 'broken window' thesis (Wilson and Kelling 1982), he starts from the assumption that minor acts or incivilities can have a spiralling effect on violence and goes on to see football hooliganism as a point of convergence for a set of closely entwined social interactions, ranging from the most innocuous to the most serious (Bodin et al. 2004b; Bodin 2008).

3.3   Theses founded on the sociology of action

The sole theory founded on the sociology of action was adopted in France by Williams Nuytens. Taking up the principle of methodological individualism posited by Raymond Boudon in the 1970s (1977, 1979), Nuytens has sought to interpret football hooliganism by looking at the interplay between the different groups of actors involved. Based on his field studies, he believes that football hooliganism is essentially a type of symbolic violent behaviour, involving intimidation and provocation, which can shift into actual violence if just a few individuals overstep the behavioural rules of the group or if there is a history of rivalry between different football supporters' groups. This latter factor, the existence of ongoing inter-group disputes, would then play a key role in the behaviour of football supporters to the extent that it also contributes to the development of the collective memory required for building a group identity. In any event, acts of violence, be they symbolic or real, are intended to provide those concerned with the social distinction and affirmation of identity desired within their peer group (2001, 2002, 2004, 2005). Having explained the hooliganism found at professional football matches in this way, Nuytens (2008) went on to look at amateur football and concluded that violence in that context was more likely to depend on certain situational factors, such as what is at stake in the match or the quality of refereeing.

While this theory is indeed original in its attempt to compare the behaviour of football supporters at both professional and amateur football matches, it does not provide a new explanation for the crowd disorder that takes place in professional football since its conclusions are similar to those reached in earlier psychological and anthropological theses on ritualized violence. Of course, it is different to the extent that it emphasizes the importance of disputes between rival football supporters' groups. However, since this aspect has already been analysed by Dal Lago and Roversi, Nuytens' works are interesting less for their originality than for the fact that, by setting out from a different perspective, they confirm some of the points made in theses developed in countries other than France.

As regards the theoretical framework chosen to explain football hooliganism, this approach undoubtedly has the merit of focusing on the individual as an actor who takes on multiple, non-predefined roles and operates within mutually dependent systems. From this point of view, it avoids the possible bias inherent in deterministic approaches but, at the same time, it also brushes aside any kind of macro-sociological view. The football supporters studied were thus very poorly related to their historical context and the analysis of their behaviour did not take account of their socio-economic or political specificities, the possible impact of social, political, economic, bureaucratic or other factors on their behaviour, or the possible interplay between the types of behaviour exhibited and the methods used to police them.

10
Legal Vagueness

In some respects, the regulation of football hooliganism has broadly evolved along the lines laid down in the preceding period. Thus, at the EU level, MEPs have continued to try to strike a balance between the principles of the risk-focused crime control policy and the protection of fundamental rights (European Parliament 2000, 2001). This position was thoroughly expounded at the 8 April 2002 sitting of the Parliament during the debate on the draft Council decision on security in connection with football matches with an international dimension, which mainly called for the creation of an EU-wide network for collecting and exchanging intelligence on football hooliganism. In fact, while some MEPs supported the introduction of proactive policing measures and did not challenge the establishment of such an extensive surveillance apparatus, others argued that, if such apparatus was to include suspected troublemakers, it would mean that deviant as well as criminal behaviour was being controlled. They therefore called for the implementation of a long-term preventive policy that could combat both social and sports-related causes of the phenomenon (European Parliament 2002). The same position was taken during the debate held on 28 March 2007 on the future of professional football in Europe and security at football matches. Although all MEPs see the establishment of an EU-wide network for collecting and exchanging intelligence as a key strategy in combating football-related violence, some insist that 'care [should] be taken when the data is being obtained. Otherwise, the national agencies might change from being tools for preventing acts of violence in stadiums into tools for social control, liable to act in an indiscriminate way' (European Parliament 2007b).

1 Multiple conceptual registers

Nevertheless, the position taken by the European Parliament remains quite marginal at the EU level. The Council of the EU has taken a significantly different stance. More specifically, while fully endorsing the principles of the risk-focused crime control policy, it has moved onto a new stage as far as defining football hooliganism is concerned, a stage that is characterized by increasing legal vagueness. The turning point was arguably the Joint Action with regard to cooperation on law and order and security, adopted in 26 May 1997 (Council of the EU 1997a). The Joint Action, which was passed without any prior consultation with the European Parliament (Statewatch 2001b), extended the provisions of the aforementioned Council Recommendation of 22 April 1996 so that they applied to public order issues in general, including those relating to sports events. It mainly provides for the collection, analysis and exchange of information on all sizeable groups that may pose a threat to law, order and security when travelling to another Member State to participate in a meeting attended by large numbers of persons from more than one Member State (Council of the EU 1997a: 1§1).[1] In order for this to be done, it stipulates that cooperation between law enforcement agencies should be further reinforced by the creation of an EU-wide pool of liaison officers (2§1).[2]

The most significant new feature of the Joint Action was the introduction of the word 'meeting' to refer to a whole array of events, ranging from sporting events to rock concerts, demonstrations and road-blocking protest campaigns. From then on, while football hooliganism, in line with the previously established perception of security threats, still formed part of the broader set of threats posed to the internal security of EU countries, it also became part of a subgroup of threats in which, in line with the principles of the risk-focused mindset, was linked to ordinary but potentially threatening collective behaviours. This classification of the phenomenon within two discrete conceptual registers indicates a profound change in its definitional process. The core components of such behaviour are still clearly circumscribed within the sphere of criminal justice, but its outer boundaries have become increasingly blurred, precisely because of its location within two distinct frames of reference. The consequences of this definitional ambiguity have moved beyond those observed in the previous period: now, potentially interconnected behaviours are no longer situated on the borderline between delinquency and deviance but on that between deviance and ordinary behaviour. What they now have in common is not the potential or effective transgression of legal or social norms but merely their propensity to create disorder, even if, strictly speaking, they do not breach any norm. The definition of the types of behaviour to be kept under control has thus been broadened once again, to include ordinary behaviours that normally fall under the remit of either legal or social norms.

The specificity of the definitional contour of football hooliganism was further weakened following the JHA Council meeting of 13 July 2001 on security at meetings of the European Council and other comparable events. The conclusions of that meeting[3] called mainly for the creation of an EU-wide network of national databases, the establishment of a pool of liaison officers and broader implementation of a measure which, prior to that, had been used solely for football hooligans, namely, the systematic use of spotters (Council of the EU 2001c: 1a, b, c). Bringing football hooliganism and demonstrations together was a key aspect of the Joint Action mentioned above. Yet the Council's conclusions introduced a new dimension because the two events were decoupled from the other high-risk behaviours referred to in the Joint Action. The association thus established between political and sports events raised the question of whether, following *mutatis mutandis* the example of football bans, individuals wishing to travel to another Member State to protest should be prevented from leaving their home country (Council of the EU 2001c: 3a). At the same time, the establishment of that particular association did not prevent football hooliganism from being further linked to other types of high-risk behaviour. Indeed, during the JHA Council meeting mentioned above, the issue was raised as to whether it was appropriate to extend the powers of Europol to cover violent disturbances, offences and groups (Council of the EU 2001c: 1e).

It is now clear that while football hooliganism already forms part of both a broad set of security threats and a subgroup of threats related to potentially dangerous collective behaviours, it is also part of a second subgroup of threats related to urban security, alongside urban riots, petty crime, juvenile delinquency and demonstrations. Locating it within yet another conceptual register not only exacerbates the splintering of its contour, so that it now comes under several categories of threat, but also significantly broadens the range of sources from which the social control apparatus can be mobilized. Having been turned into a fluid concept revolving around a solid core of punishable behaviours, and being subject to *de facto* delimitations without having been properly defined in law, football hooliganism, depending on how it is classified in any given context, ends up acquiring some of the features of the behaviours it is associated with. How it is classified, in turn, justifies the implementation of certain specific security measures deemed capable of addressing one or more specific aspects of the phenomenon.

In 2001, this trend was further consolidated when the Council stated, in the Resolution of 6 December, that national football information points could, should the need arise, exchange information regarding other matters besides sporting events (annexe: ch. 1, s. 2). Reiterated in the Council Resolution of 4 December 2006 (annexe: ch. 1, s. 2), this provision was criticized by the European Parliament in its legislative Resolution of 29 March 2007. However, this had no effect on the position of the Council, which, in its Decision of 12 June 2007, failed to impose any limitations on the exchange of information. The exchange of intelligence on known or potential troublemakers crossing national frontiers to attend sporting events or in connection with European Council's meetings was also included in the Treaty of Prüm (2005: arts. 13–14) while, in 2006, a note from the Presidency of the Council provided for a security handbook to be used by police authorities and services at international events, whether political, sporting, social, cultural or other, to address public order as well as counter-terrorism issues (Council of the EU 2006b).

At the conceptual level, the common denominator of these multiple classifications is that they are grouped under the heading of 'conflict'. In a preliminary note for an experts' meeting convened by the JHA Council in 1998,[4] conflict was defined as any act contrary to the public's perception of normality or which adversely affects their quality of life (Council of the EU 1998: 3.1). Consequently, it is broad enough to include both crime and disorder. The ensuing blurring of the boundaries between delinquency, deviance and ordinary behaviour is not founded on any kind of legal concept, but on an essentially political one, since the note specifies that conflict has the potential to have an adverse effect on the status quo (Council of the EU 1998: 3.2). This restrictive definition of conflict, which focuses on its potential for causing disorder and destruction but disregards its positive contribution to social life, brings together a broad-ranging set of behaviours to be kept under control through the implementation of anticipatory patterns of action that seek to identify and control tensions within society (Council of the EU 1998: 3.3).

The gradual replacement of the legal term 'offence' by the political one 'conflict' as one of the grounds justifying mobilization of the social control apparatus was further confirmed by the Council Decision of 28 May 2001 on setting up a European crime prevention network. In fact, the definition contained in the proposal put forward by the European Commission for decision by the Council, stating that the concept of crime could also cover anti-social conduct which, without necessarily being a criminal offence, by its cumulative effect could generate a climate of tension and insecurity (European Commission 2000: art. 2.2.1), was not taken up by the authors of the above-mentioned

Council Decision. However, they did not entirely remove the political element from their own definition of the types of behaviour to be controlled because they specified that crime prevention should intend to reduce or otherwise contribute to reducing crime and citizens' sense of insecurity (Council of the EU 2001a: art. 1.3). Behaviour such as football hooliganism has thus been reframed around a solid core of legal and political concepts, which justify its control on the grounds of protecting both public and political order. This is clearly illustrated by the Council's vague definition of a 'risk supporter' as a person who 'can be regarded as posing a possible risk to public order or to antisocial behaviour' (Council of the EU 2006c: app. 1).

Since the feeling of insecurity is closely related to a series of social, political and economic factors, which cannot be dissociated from numerous political stakes, the grounds for mobilizing the social control apparatus are now potentially infinite. Yet, however practical it may seem to law enforcement agents, framing football hooliganism in this way makes it fully controllable and uncontrollable at the same time. In fact, the multiple positioning of the phenomenon at the conceptual level, at the same time as exponentially enhancing the possibilities and modes of intervention of the social control apparatus, also magnifies the scale of football hooliganism to such an extent that it turns it into a boundless problem, a protean security threat that will eventually escape all control. While the establishment of football information points in every Member State for exchanging information and facilitating international police cooperation in connection with football matches (provided in the Council Decision of 25 April 2002) may thus seem necessary to deal with such a threat, it nevertheless still fails to encompass the whole spectrum of football hooliganism. It remains, by definition, a temporary phase in a permanently evolving control apparatus which, always at some point in the future, will be deemed inefficient and therefore need to be strengthened to better cope with the threat.

Of course, this continual strengthening of the counter-hooliganism security apparatus does not always mean that the control of deviance is also being strengthened. While the Council Resolution of 17 November 2003 on Member States' use of bans on access to football match venues with an international dimension invited Member States to examine the possibility of introducing both domestic and international football bans, it specified that this provision should apply only to persons previously found guilty of violent conduct at football matches (art. 1, 3). By contrast, Council Decision 2006/ . . . /JHA amending Decision 2002/348/JHA concerning security in connection with football matches with an international dimension empowered national football information points to collect and exchange personal data not only on high-risk supporters, as provided by Decision 2002/348/JHA, but also on those associated with lower risk (art. 1.1a). The subsequent expansion of the control of deviance was further confirmed by the call for national football information points to produce and diffuse regular generic and/or thematic national football disorder assessments (art. 1.1b).

The importance accorded to the notion of threat when defining football hooliganism has also ended up changing the way decision-makers think. Indeed, given that this notion has an intrinsic element of potentiality since it consists of predicting the future evolution of harm that has already occurred, the assertion of its existence and its undisputed gravity means that this element of potentiality is now being amplified in order to encompass the past also. Thus, in 1999, the author of a report prepared by the Council of Europe's Committee on Culture and Education gave an account of the law enforcement policies applied during international tournaments. Believing that all official reports on past incidents lacked objectivity and sought to minimize football-related incidents, he maintained that it was necessary for analysis not to be confined to looking at the incidents that had taken place, but to consider those which had not (Council of Europe 1999a: D.41).

This position, which is entirely consistent with the rationale of the risk-focused mindset, has reinforced the ambiguity of the role played by the Council of Europe with regard to civil liberties. This ambiguity, which was evident as early as 1985 when the Council abandoned its role as the guardian of human rights in order to institutionalize the control of deviance for the first time, persisted throughout the 1980s and 1990s, a period during which it seemed to be concerned about football hooliganism solely as a public order problem.[5]

In fact, racist incidents involving football supporters only elicited a specific reaction from the Council in 2000 when it passed Resolution No. 4 on preventing racism, xenophobia and intolerance in sport. A year later, in Recommendation Rec(2001)6 on the prevention of racism, xenophobia and racial intolerance in sport, it established the broad outlines of its first comprehensive policy on the issue and called for tougher penalties for football supporters and players as well as the sporting bodies involved (Council of Europe 2001: B, C, E) and the introduction of a long-term preventive policy inside and outside sports venues (Council of Europe 2001: E, F, G). As far as combating homophobia in stadia was concerned, this was not addressed until 2003 (Council of Europe 2003b).

Though slow in coming, these initiatives clearly demonstrate that the Council of Europe is actively protecting democratic order within its Member States. However, such protection has been undermined by its failure to challenge the validity of introducing control and surveillance devices for use against football supporters, a failing that has had detrimental consequences for civil liberties. For example, the authors of the 2001 Recommendation requested that video cameras and CCTV systems installed in stadia for public safety and public order reasons also be used to assist to identify racist offenders (Council of Europe 2001: D.2) and that efforts to stamp out racism be strengthened by providing for strict penalties and even non-penal sanctions, such as exclusion or banning from football stadia (C.4).

2 Football bans 'on suspicion'

The consequences of classifying football hooliganism under multiple conceptual registers are already visible at the national level. Although control and surveillance devices were essentially already in place during the preceding period, the conversion of the football banning order from ordinary penalty to a risk management tool seems to be a clear translation to the national level of the changes to the definitional frame of football hooliganism that have taken place at the transnational level. Apart from Italy where, as early as 1989, administrative football bans were provided in law,[6] the football banning orders introduced in several European countries during the preceding period[7] were initially imposed by the courts on conviction as an additional penalty and were in principle national in scope. They applied to all stadia within a given country and the most common way of ensuring their enforcement was to require the person subject to a football ban to attend at a police station for a specific period on the day of the match.

In the late 1990s, however, the use of administrative football bans, based on reports compiled by police officers, started to spread slowly across Europe.[8] Of variable duration, such bans were initially applicable only nationally. The next turning point came in Germany where, with Euro 2000 imminent, the authorities amended the law on passports and banned some 60 known football hooligans from leaving the country. In the same year, the Football (Disorder) Act 2000 substantially amended football banning orders in the UK by broadening their scope and their legal basis. Applicable both nationally and abroad, they now entail a series of constraints: at the national level, ranging from requiring the person concerned to attend at a police station for the duration of a match to banning them from using public transport on match days and/or from visiting town centres, pubs and bars during risk periods; as far as attending matches abroad is concerned, they involve preventing people from leaving the UK by forcing them to surrender their passports for a specific period. Football banning orders are imposed by a magistrates' court or by the Crown Court following conviction for a public order offence,[9] or by a magistrates' court, in accordance with the civil procedure rules, following submission of a complaint by the police or the Crown Prosecution Service.[10] In the latter case, a complaint may be brought if the claimant can satisfy the court that the individual concerned has at any time caused or contributed to any violence or disorder in the UK or elsewhere.

In France, Law 2006–64 of 23 January 2006 on the fight against terrorism enabled the authorities to prohibit entry into stadia, for a maximum of three months, of anyone whose behaviour has been deemed to threaten public order during a sporting event. In August 2007, Circular INT/D/07/00089/C on the implementation of administrative football banning orders specified that the conduct being penalized by such orders did not have to constitute a criminal offence; it was sufficient for it to amount to 'behaviour that is generally threatening to public order'. As the original length of such banning orders is now deemed to be insufficient, a Parliamentary Report is currently recommending it be increased to six months (Assemblée Nationale 2007) while the authors of a recent Senate Report want it increased to a whole year (Sénat 2007: 36).

The rapid proliferation in the use of such bans marks a turning point in the repression of football hooliganism. People can now be deprived of their freedom of movement, within their own country or abroad, and subjected to other types of constraints on the basis of suspicion alone. Furthermore, they are effectively punished twice. In addition to the initial penalty – namely, the limiting of their freedom of movement within a given area for a specific period of time – there is a 'hidden' penalty that is likely to be applied for much longer within a potentially much broader arena. This 'hidden' penalty stems from the way intelligence agencies operate. To be more specific, the fact that they usually store their data for at least five years means that the initial penalty is subject to a virtual prolongation which, based on the suspicion thus established, can have real consequences well after the initial penalty has expired. For example, Belgian football supporters who had had three-month administrative banning orders imposed on them in the early 2000s were turned away at the German border or deported from German territory during the 2006

World Cup. It is worth remembering here that the national authorities have, in this instance, no room for manœuvre because, according to the Council Resolution of 17 November 2003 (art. 5), information on football bans issued domestically has to be given to countries staging international football matches.

The swift spread of these non-penal sanctions to many different European countries is of concern in many respects. First, the implicit replacement of the judiciary by the executive raises, above all, a political problem because it calls into question the principle of the separation of powers. In fact, the expansion of the executive at the expense of the other two powers is nothing new in itself and the resulting confusion between the roles of the different powers is one of the direct consequences of the use of surveillance devices (De Valkeneer 1990: 323) and proactive control measures in general. In the case of football hooliganism in particular, since the 1970s such confusion has been evident when people have been arrested for being involved in football-related incidents (Trivizas 1980, 1984; Williams 1980). However, until now, this has usually been due to the way the police operate and, to a certain extent, was a perverse effect of policies which otherwise complied with democratic standards. These days, on the contrary, the separation of powers is being deliberately flouted by the legislator who, in institutionalizing the confusion, is fully accepting its consequences. This attack on the foundations of democratic government is all the more serious in that this undermining of a democratic principle goes hand in hand with a challenge to one of the principles of the rule of law, since the imposition of penalties involving the loss of liberty outside the framework of a criminal trial may constitute a breach of the principle of presumption of innocence.

The idea that such penalties might contravene the legal order of the countries concerned has, nevertheless, not been accepted by national judges. For example, in Belgium, the Court of Arbitration, in its decision 175/2002 of 5 December 2002 in answer to an interlocutory question posed by the Court of First Instance in Criminal Matters of Turnhout, ruled that, regardless of whether or not the administrative proceedings in question were legally valid, an immediate three-month banning order did not constitute a penalty but was a preventive security measure. Furthermore, given the very limited length and scope of the football ban, as well as the procedural guarantees applicable to it,[11] the court deemed that its imposition did not entail a breach of articles 10 and 11 of the Belgian Constitution, which guarantee equal rights and no discrimination, or article 6.1 of the European Convention on Human Rights, which guarantees the right to a fair trial. This Belgian court ruling is broadly similar to one handed down in the UK on 13 July 2001 by a magistrates' court, which took the view that, even if they did possess a punitive element, football banning orders on complaint did not seek to inflict punishment but to protect the public by preventative measures.[12]

However, it should be stated that, in practice, people who have been hit with 'football bans on suspicion' have their freedom of movement inside their home country or abroad restricted, a penalty which, as a rule, is imposed with none of the procedural guarantees provided by the criminal justice system (Pearson 2005; Blackshaw 2005; Stott and Pearson 2006). In addition, as noted above, such people are doubly punished due to the fact that their personal data are entered into police files. From the legal standpoint, given the fact that the European Court of Human Rights has constantly stipulated that, in order to prevent the disciplinary from encroaching illegally on the criminal justice realm, punitive measures should be defined in law according to their effect (Delmas-Marty 2002: 448ff), a challenge to the claim that this type of measure is not a penalty could be brought before it. From a criminological point of view, denying that this type of measure is a penalty raises the question of how 'penalty' is defined in the current era of social control.

In fact, the introduction of these penalties marks a turning point in the attitude of the social control apparatus to deviant groups. In line with the institutionalization of the control of deviance that stems from the adoption of the risk-focused crime management model, this approach no longer simply seeks to alter the existing scope of the control of deviance and the forms it takes. It now goes beyond making such alterations to establishing a system of direct punishment for deviant individuals. Just as we have seen in connection with the separation of powers, the punishment of deviance is no longer a possible indirect consequence of the tightening of the control of deviance but explicitly a quasi-ordinary penalty. The legislature and the executive therefore do not now have to compete to define the boundaries of (il)legality and the penalties to be imposed on offenders. However, this seems to have been achieved at the expense of the rule of law. In this context, it is indeed possible to see these punitive measures as not being penalties; however, this just shows that the standard definition of the term 'penalty' no longer covers this type of proactive punishment which, bearing in mind that its intention is to manage deviance by eliminating or changing socially unacceptable conduct, could be described as 'disciplinary punishment'.

Even though it received official backing from both the EU bodies (European Parliament 2000: art. 5; Council of the EU 2003, 2007b: annex 42, 44) and UEFA (Chaplin 2007), this conversion of the football banning order into a risk management tool also seems to run counter to three other principles of law. First, it may constitute a breach of the principle of proportionality to the extent that, in the absence of any legal assessment of the dangerousness of the behaviour being penalized, in the case of France, or following a cursory legal assessment, in the case of the UK (Mark and Pearson 2006; Stott and Pearson 2007: 190ff), it is impossible to establish with any certainty that the limitations imposed on individual rights are necessary for the protection of collective interests or that the individual rights being limited are less important than the social values being protected (Pearson 2005). Second, this uncertainty also calls into question the validity of restricting freedom of movement within the EU which, under Community law, is only legal if done in response to national security needs and is proportionate to the seriousness of the problem in question. Lastly, in the case of the UK in particular, the fact that football banning orders can be imposed as a result of two types of proceedings may amount to a breach of the right to a fair trial since the weight of evidence required to bring a charge varies according to whether the proceedings in question take place in a criminal or civil court (Pearson 2005).

While the introduction of these penalties raises numerous political and legal problems in the countries concerned, their systematic use could also raise a question with regard to the interpretation of Community law since it results in the *de facto* institutionalization of the reintroduction of border controls in the Schengen area. Actually, this reintroduction of border controls, used for the first time in a sports context during Euro 2000, has been common practice among Member States since the late 1990s. In 2001, the European Parliament was already drawing attention to the fact that frequent recourse to this practice was a denial of the derogatory nature of article 2.2. of the Schengen Convention. It also complained that an exceptional provision had been turned into a general rule that was at the disposal of governments whenever they feared crowd disorder, even for international events of minor importance (European Parliament 2001: 5.1). Still, formally speaking, Member States that are hosting international events at which crowd disorder is anticipated are free to take other steps to protect security and public order that do not involve imposing border controls. This flexibility in decision-making has, however, totally vanished in the case of football hooliganism since, in order for international football bans to be effectively enforced, by definition, border controls have to be re-established during international tournaments.[13]

While, as already mentioned, the spread of 'football bans on suspicion' raises a series of legal and political problems affecting both domestic and EU law, the constant evolution of football hooliganism arguably raises a further legal question with regard to the scope of domestic counter-hooliganism laws. As described earlier, these have usually been structured around a spatial criterion, frequently formulated as 'at, or in connection with, football matches', which has quickly come to be interpreted flexibly to include pre- and post-match football-related incidents. Yet this criterion can no longer be assumed to apply when football hooligans engage in pre-arranged fights at times and places that are unrelated to any sports event. The fact that, as a direct consequence of the absence of a legal definition of football hooliganism, counter-hooliganism legislation is still applied in such unclear situations, thus only further contributes to the above-mentioned splintering of the definition of the phenomenon.

11
The Decompartmentalization of Policing

During this period, while the policing of football hooliganism has certainly been characterized by the widespread continuation of the main trends from the previous period, it has at the same time gone down new avenues to the extent that it has reflected a tendency for internal and external security agencies to become entangled (Bigo 2000, 2001) and for policing methods and practices to become decompartmentalized.

The perception of global threat has been spreading so quickly that it is now commonplace for the boundaries between deviant and criminal behaviours and between criminal phenomena generally to become blurred, while the numbers of security professionals who think in terms of there being interconnected networks of transnational threats is snowballing. At the moment, it is broadly accepted that these proliferating threats are being produced by people whom it is hard or even impossible to define by applying the main criteria used in the past[1] and who are seen as dangerous precisely because they are embedded within a vague, mutating and loose frame of reference. The influence of this dominant perception of threat is seen clearly in the wording of the Council Resolution of 9 June 1997 mentioned above, which, despite the absence of any evidence to substantiate the existence of international hooligan networks, stated that 'special attention shall be given to the international networks of supporters' groups concerned' (Council of the EU 1997b: art. 2).

1 Crossing over lines

The search for effective ways to address this type of threat quite naturally hastened the ongoing transfer of practices from other areas of policing and further enhanced international cooperation. Faced with a set of threats which were seen as intermingled, hard to locate and difficult to control, it seemed essential to decompartmentalize knowledge, bring services together and allow everyone to benefit from the experience already acquired within any specific field of police activity. It therefore hardly came as a surprise when, at the time of the 1998 World Cup, the French authorities resorted to using a measure that up to then had been reserved solely for combating terrorism, namely, the immediate issuing of deportation orders against certain football supporters who, no sooner had they arrived on French territory, were identified by spotters as constituting a potential risk to the security of the country.

Taking a similar approach, the conclusions of the JHA Council meeting of 13 July 2001 suggested using spotters to ensure security at meetings of the European Council and other comparable events. The proposing of this measure, which is in fact not very effective for dealing with large crowds, was a clear indication that combating football hooliganism was no longer simply an area into which policing methods were being imported from other domains, but had now become a laboratory for testing and exporting new internal security methods. For example, as soon as it had entered into force in May 2000, the amended German law on passports, which prohibited certain troublemakers wanting to go to Euro 2000 from leaving the country, was also used against people who were planning to go to Genoa at the time of the G8 Summit to participate in the anti-globalization protests there (European Parliament 2002).

This unleashing into the security realm of counter-hooliganism policies has been largely facilitated by the recurrent nature of the organization of international tournaments which has meant that police cooperation and cooperation among security agencies and the judiciary has advanced at a much faster pace than in many other areas. At the moment, these tournaments are being used as experimental sites for the large-scale testing of new strategies and tactics on crowd control and cooperation among social control agents which can later be applied to other fields of activity. For example, at the time of the 1998 World Cup, experts thought that the repressive apparatus introduced to deal with football hooligans should be used in future for suppressing urban riots (Richard 1998), while the establishment, by the two host countries of Euro 2000, of a coordination and cooperation system involving security agents from sixteen European countries was seen as a model for improving European understanding (Broussard 2000).

Against this background of increased cooperation, in 2001 the Belgian authorities proposed setting up a network of national intelligence agencies on football hooliganism, data from which would be incorporated into what was to become SIS II.[2] At first, this proposal was heavily criticized by several European countries[3] which, on the one hand, did not want to have to introduce an onerous system, the effectiveness of which would in fact be very limited, and, on the other, believed that the measure took very little account of conditions specific at the national level. For example, it was argued that, while keeping files on known football hooligans might be effective in Germany, for instance, where 'once a hooligan, always a hooligan', it was not as appropriate in England, where there was the potential for any football supporter to be involved in violence, and completely unsuited to the situation in Greece, where participating in football hooliganism was seen as part of the standard rite of passage into adulthood and ceased when adolescence came to an end. This measure was viewed as all the more irrelevant in that it took no account of national differences in the level of involvement of football supporters in incidents abroad, which was very high in the case of English and German hooligans but very low in the case of the Dutch, Italian, Greek and French, for example. These reservations were, nevertheless, brushed aside once and for all in April 2002 with the EU-wide establishment of national football information points for coordinating and facilitating the exchange of relevant information between law enforcement agencies in connection with football matches with an international dimension (Council of the EU 2002b).

This expansion of the surveillance apparatus went far beyond simply broadening its scope in terms of size. By increasing the likelihood that breaches of the fundamental freedoms of the football supporters concerned would be committed, since it also applied to potential troublemakers, it normalized the institutionalization of the control of deviance at the EU level. The enshrinement of the principles of actuarial risk management that this Decision implied was further confirmed by the position the Council took with regard to the introduction, safeguarding and exchange of the personal data contained in such files. While the Council Resolution of 6 December 2001 devoted much attention to how these national football information points would operate, how the files would be controlled was given only a cursory mention, in the following terms: 'the exchange of personal information is subject to the applicable national and international law' (Council of the EU 2002a: IV.1b). Council Decision of 25 April 2002 further specified that the exchange of personal data should take account of the principles of

Convention No. 108 of the Council of Europe of 28 January 1981 and, where appropriate, Recommendation No. R (87)15 of the Committee of Ministers of the Council of Europe of 17 September 1987 (art. 3.3).[4] However, since this protection cannot ensure effective control of either the criteria for entering personal data on potential troublemakers or police methods of keeping and exchanging personal data, it cannot ensure that the rights of individuals are defended against the control of deviance thereby established.

The Council's position also seems to be prevalent among MEPs. In fact, when invited to vote on the above-mentioned draft Council decision proposing the establishment of national football information points in all Member States, the majority unreservedly endorsed this approach. For example, the Rapporteur, Gérard Deprez, said that 'in order to prevent disturbances and to maintain law and order in connection with football matches, it is essential to have, first and foremost, an organized and efficient system for exchanging information' (European Parliament 2002). With the exception of the interventions of two MEPs, who raised the question of the lack of democratic control over these police structures and the threat to human rights posed by the new measure, its validity was hardly discussed, the majority of the debate focusing solely on the possibility of improving its effectiveness.

Since optimum management of the information passed between domestic intelligence agencies requires the establishment of a coordination centre, there are now plans to broaden the powers of the European Police Office in order to facilitate future development of counter-hooliganism security policies. Already outlined in the conclusions of the JHA Council meeting of 13 July 2001, which proposed that the powers of Europol be extended to cover violent disturbances, offences and groups (Council of the EU 2001c: 1e), the broadening of Europol's mandate is currently under discussion following the presentation of a draft proposal by the European Commission on 20 December 2006, calling for the gathering and analysis of information to be permitted in order to ensure public order during, among other events, international football matches (art. 5.1–f).

The involvement of Europol and Eurojust in the fight against football hooliganism, which received strong backing from the European Commission in November 2007 (Frattini 2007), is now being accompanied by enhanced training for police and other security agents. The training, which is coordinated by Europol, is partly funded by the European Community. This determination to standardize the policing of football hooliganism as much as possible, which is also clearly evident in the pivotal, EU-wide role the EU Council has given a group of police experts,[5] was also behind the recent call by the European Commission and UEFA for the creation of a European Sports Police Force, responsible, among other things, for combating football-related violence.

2 Reintroducing the human factor

Though now dominant, this counter-hooliganism policy coexists in parallel with another model that has been very successfully applied during some recent international tournaments.[6] Drafted and developed in the Netherlands in the lead-up to Euro 2000, what is usually referred to as 'friendly but firm' policing (Adang and Cuvelier 2001) is currently founded on a dual premise. On the one hand, it adopts a risk-focused approach during the preparatory stages of a tournament in that it relies heavily on proactive policing; on the other hand, it breaks with the impersonal nature of risk-oriented strategies and reintroduces the human factor during the tournament when law enforcers and football supporters come face to face. To do so, it relies on drawing a clear line between football hooligans and the vast majority of peaceful football supporters, thereby resulting in the *a priori* friendly handling of the latter in a festive atmosphere, based on the establishment of a certain degree of mutual trust within the parameters of a predetermined threshold of tolerance.

Yet however significant this break with the dominant, risk-focused style of policing may be, the fact that the confrontational approach to dealing with a supposedly hostile crowd has been rejected and that it is now accepted that the crowd to be controlled comprises *a priori* law-abiding individuals has not brought about a reversal of the dominant trend. On the contrary, it has even indirectly validated it to the extent that the 'friendly but firm' policing of football supporters is supposedly possible only once the 'risk supporters' have been removed, thanks precisely to the use of proactive risk management measures.

Justified on the grounds that football hooliganism is a threat to the development of the EU as an area of freedom, justice and security (Council of the EU 2003: Preamble), or even the development of the European idea and solidarity within the EU (European Parliament 2000: F), the repeated stress placed on the use of such control and surveillance apparatuses in dealing with football supporters can, of course, easily be explained to the extent that it is consistent with the collective and anticipatory nature of the actuarial risk management methods that are currently prevalent.

Still, the resultant calling into question of the rule of law and civil liberties seems, at the same time, to be closely bound up with the incessant (re)configuration of the political field. Earlier research revealed that attempts to subordinate civil liberties to security are often a way for the executive to disguise its desire to shift the balance of power between it and the judiciary and/or civil society and to redefine the subjects of law by controlling and excluding certain social groups (Tsoukala 2004a, 2006a, 2006c, 2008a). However, this attempt by the state to express its sovereign authority by designating populations to be targeted by social control and the executive's desire to assert and even strengthen its position within the political field usually encounter opposition from other actors in the same field, namely, the political class and/or civil society. Thus, in the context of contemporary liberal democracies, efforts by the executive to stigmatize and criminalize certain social groups, and even to set up parallel criminal justice systems in the name of protecting internal security, have been systematically denounced and, at least in part, thwarted by numerous actors from the political field. And yet, in the case of football hooliganism, this democratic balancing act seems to have been virtually absent, with the establishment of control and surveillance apparatuses having been accepted without much opposition from not only the political class but also civil society within the countries concerned. Apart from an occasional reaction in the UK or Italy, for example, where the infringement of the civil liberties of football supporters has mobilized some human rights groups (Liberty 2000; Statewatch 2001a), football supporters' organizations (Progetto ultra) and football supporters' groups (Louis 2006: 141–3), the establishment and ongoing strengthening of these control and surveillance measures have been greeted with general indifference. It is revealing in this regard that the introduction of administrative football bans in France attracted very little media coverage and, in particular, prompted no protests from human rights organizations. The holding of the 2006 World Cup in Germany could have marked a turning point in this respect since it saw the emergence of a group of sporting, cultural and political organizations that denounced, among other things, the breaching of the rights of football supporters as a result of the implementation of a tougher control and surveillance apparatus.[7] However, despite its size, this movement received very little media coverage outside of Germany.[8]

This indifference on the part of civil society is all the more serious because it is accompanied by a longstanding indifference on the part of the authorities to the football supporters' world. Up till now, football supporters' organizations have indeed been invited to cooperate with public and sports authorities,[9] but they have not been involved in devising the framework within which this cooperation takes place. On the contrary, all attempts on their part to become actively involved in designing counter-hooliganism policies have been met with great suspicion by public and sports authorities as well as the media. For example, the Football Supporters' Association has been waiting for years for their members' ideas about organizing international tournaments to be actively supported by officials,[10] while the goodwill actions undertaken by small groups of football supporters in countries staging international tournaments[11] are hardly ever covered by the media in their countries of origin, which seem *de facto* reluctant to see the prevailing image of the 'dangerous football supporter' change.

This failure to counterbalance or delimit the power of the executive in managing football hooliganism, by definition, leaves the way open for all kinds of possible excesses on the part of the actors responsible for controlling the phenomenon, whether they be from the security or the sporting field. For example, believing that the civilian law enforcement agencies would be unable to deal with football hooliganism effectively, the organizers of the 2006 World Cup also called in the military. At first sight, this request was not so unusual since the military had already been called in during the 1990 and 1998 World Cups, in Italy and France respectively, in order to provide logistical support to the tournament organizers. Far from being out of the ordinary, this involvement of the military in the management of football hooliganism reflects the growing role played in protecting internal security by the armed forces who, anxious to hold on to their budgets and personnel in the post-Cold War era, have gradually taken on tasks related to the control of national territory (Bigo 1999, 2000, 2001; Tsoukala 2004c).

This convergence of the internal and external security realms, which was consolidated and amplified following the terrorist attacks of 11 September 2001, has found itself a regular field of application in major international sporting events, where the increased security requirements have obliged the organizers to call on the military for support, but now it is happening at transnational level, with NATO being called in. Already called on during Euro 2004 and the 2004 Olympic Games (Tsoukala 2006d), NATO was again asked to help with security protection during the 2006 World Cup. However, while the support it gave the Portuguese and Greek organizers entailed a set of counterterrorist measures, the support requested of it by the organizers of the 2006 World Cup was radically different because it also explicitly targeted football hooligans. In fact, although the German government had recourse to the national army, which was responsible for providing logistical support but was also ready to intervene in the event of serious public order problems, it requested that NATO put a squadron of Awacs surveillance aircraft at its disposal in order to enhance protection against terrorist attacks during the tournament. At the same time, the crew of these aircraft were asked to use their sophisticated radar detection system to monitor the movements of football hooligans and provide police with an early warning of any suspicious crowd build-up (Hughes 2005). This revealed a new approach to the design of football hooliganism control apparatuses on the part of government and sports officials who, under the joint influence of the global threat perception and the increased importance of actuarial risk management principles, are trying to eliminate the risk of football hooliganism without taking into account the nature or proportionality of the apparatus used to do so, or the impact it might have on the civil rights and liberties of the people it is targeting.

12
The Consensus around Security

The growing importance of security's place on the post-Cold War political agenda has quite clearly led to a significant transformation of the media representation of football hooliganism. While confirming the findings of some British studies (Armstrong 1998: 85–104; Weed 2001; Poulton 2002, 2005), which reveal that the UK media image of football hooliganism continues to rely on a binary representation of the issue, my own analysis of the quality press coverage from the UK, France, Italy, Greece and Belgium[1] further shows that this way of representing the issue now predominates in many European countries and that this stereotyped representation of the phenomenon is accompanied by an increased emphasis on upholding the value of security (Tsoukala, 2004b, 2006b). Now omnipresent, the value of security is indisputable: it transcends countries and political divisions, disregards or discredits any conflicting views and justifies the adoption of whatever measures are deemed necessary to protect it, even at the expense of civil liberties.

1 Sustaining the image of the 'dangerous football hooligan'

Comparison of the findings obtained by examining the situation in each country reveals that the perpetuation of the image of the 'dangerous football hooligan' has been assured by the now widespread adherence to a strict binary logic based on the key patterns of representation observed in the previous periods. The image of anti-social and pathological/irrational behaviour is thus regularly bolstered by comments describing football hooliganism as 'senseless fury' (*Guardian*, 18 June 2002: 6) or a 'scourge' (*Libre Belgique*, 10 May 2002)[2] and football hooligans as 'uncontrollable criminal elements' (*Kyriakatiki Eleftherotypia*, 12 March 2000: 125) and 'terrorists' (*Eleftherotypia*, 1 November

2003: 66), or 'brainless' (*Nea*, 18–19 November 2000: 58), 'warp-minded' (*Guardian*, 20 June 2000: 21), 'empty-headed' (*La Stampa*, 18 November 2007: 32) and 'simpletons and cretins' (*Guardian*, 20 June 2000: 22).

Such stigmatizing terms now often appear even in the main headlines of the quality press which, given its regular use of sensational photos, is increasingly indistinguishable from the tabloids. Commonly describing football hooligans as 'thugs' (*Guardian*, 20 June 2000: 1) and football hooliganism as a 'disease' (*Independent*, 20 June 2000: 5; *Guardian*, 20 May 2002: 10), a 'social pathology' (*Libération*, 16 June 1998: 2), a type of 'fury' (*La Repubblica*, 18 June 2000: 1) or 'terror' (*Kyriakatiki Eleftherotypia*, 7 December 1997: 104–5), it now has no hesitation in resorting to war metaphors. By accentuating the contrast between the violence of football hooliganism and the supposedly peaceful nature of the society in which it takes place, headlines such as 'soccer war' (*The Observer*, 4 June 2000: 16; *Corriere della Sera*, 24 November 2007: 10) and 'English invasion' (*Guardian*, 12 June 2000: 2) only increase the public's anxiety about this undeclared war which, as it seems to be never-ending, can only be damaging to social peace in the long term.

This qualitative upgrading of the use of stigmatizing terms has resulted in them becoming commonplace – a process which has been further facilitated by the fact that they are increasingly used by sports officials, senior government representatives and even academics. Thus, while the president of UEFA calls football hooliganism a 'social scourge' (Chaplin 2008), the vice-president of the Belgian Football Federation describes football hooligans as 'unbalanced' (*Libre Belgique*, 5 February 2007),[3] a French academic claims they are 'mentally deficient both intellectually and emotionally' (A. Philonenko, in *Le Figaro*, 23 June 1998: 9C), the British prime minister talks about 'mindless thuggery' (*The Times*, 19 June 2000: 1) which 'bring[s] disgrace to our country' (*Independent*, 20 June 2000: 1), the British Home Secretary refers to 'drunken thuggery' (*Guardian*, 19 June 2000: 3), and his French counterpart says they are 'thugs' who should be severely punished (*Le Monde*, 25 January 2003: 8).

The dangerousness of this type of irrational behaviour is further strengthened by another strategy that seeks to put forward a 'Jekyll and Hyde' image of football supporters. This representation does not base their dangerousness on their 'otherness' but on the criminal nature of individuals who behave in that way because they either enjoy violence or want to goad the authorities. It does not see football hooligans as suffering the effects of any kind of socio-economic exclusion; quite the reverse, they are people who are reasonably well established in life and are simply looking for some kind of adventure, a source of excitement and/or an outlet for their hostility towards law enforcement officials. They are therefore a threat because of their criminal mentality and their willingness to transgress social norms. So press reports focus on 'surprisingly middle-aged and well-heeled' fans (*Independent*, 19 June 2000: 3) in order to show that allegedly respectable and comfortably off citizens regularly turn into violent thugs (*Le Monde*, 23 June 1998: II; *Le Soir*, 23 June 2000).[4]

These increasingly frequent assertions concerning the social origin of football hooligans seem, however, to belong to the realm of ideological construction rather than that of neutral public information. In fact, far from referring to academic studies, they extrapolate from police reports on football supporters who have been arrested for hooliganism, usually abroad. Yet such information can be erroneous if, as has often been the case, law enforcement agents arrest and deport football supporters indiscriminately. Furthermore, these claims about the mixed social origin of football hooligans confuse social origin and social position since, on the one hand, they conceal the fact that football hooligans from different social backgrounds can still occupy a very low social position within their respective countries and, on the other, they focus solely on whether or not they are in employment, without considering how secure their work may be. Needless to say, the diffusion of this image implicitly backs up the irrationality thesis since such violent behaviour would seem to indicate a deviation from an otherwise normal life which for every individual constitutes their greatest innermost fear, namely that of falling victim to uncontrollable impulses, and for every social group embodies the enormous threat facing them, namely that of regularly falling victim to such 'meaningless' violence.

However meaningless it may be perceived to be, such violence is bound up with other aggravating factors, which are usually only superficially addressed. In addition to the pervasiveness of heavy drinking, the most frequently mentioned factors affecting the behaviour of football supporters are their search for visibility, manifested in their willingness to fight to defend their 'colours' or territory, thereby proving their existence, and their racist and nationalist sentiments (*Le Monde*, 16 June 1998: I; *Guardian*, 18 June 2002: 6), which are regularly stoked by tabloid discourses.

In all cases, the reporting of these supposedly aggravating factors, which further relies on divorcing football hooligans from 'genuine supporters' (*Guardian*, 20 June 2000: 1, 8 August 2005: 19; *Kyriakatiki Eleftherotypia*, 12 March 2000: 125; *Corriere della Sera*, 17 February

2007: 10), is never accompanied by any socio-political analysis of the phenomenon. Therefore, except for the frequent allegations of collusion between football hooligans and club officials in Greece and Italy, violent football supporters are seen as linked to their historical context either as the negative expression of the growing spectacularization of social life or as alleged holders of extremist political beliefs, if not the passive tools of a tabloid-fuelled chauvinist and xenophobic ideology. This reality-reducing representation, which has been observed in many studies of the media coverage of various types of criminal behaviour related to social tensions (Champagne 1991; Schneider 1992: 92; Schlesinger and Tumber 1994: 204; Peralva and Macé 2002; Welch et al. 2002), is, of course, entirely consistent with the earlier methods employed to discursively construct threat. However, it has, at the same time, become increasingly less possible to challenge it, insofar as it is consistent with the guiding principles of the risk-focused crime control model which rejects as inappropriate any consideration of social factors when seeking to control crime. The existence of this implicit ideological consensus among journalists, law enforcers and politicians with regard to the understanding of the origins, nature and social impact of football hooliganism thus merely reinforces the generation of a stereotyped discourse which, in giving the public the pleasure of feeling they belong to a large community that shares the same view of the world as far as social order is concerned (Peelo and Soothill 2000; Luhmann 2003: 74–5, 150ff), appears legitimate in their eyes precisely because of the absence of any counter-discourse.[5]

Once it had been defined in that way, the threat that football hooliganism supposedly represented for the security of the societies concerned was regularly amplified using the same methods as in the preceding two periods. The aim of such amplification is, first of all, to ensure that the threat seems credible, something that relies not only on football hooliganism being seen as an ongoing problem but also football-related incidents appearing to be frequent. In the former case, the enduring nature of the phenomenon is insinuated by publishing lists of the major incidents that have taken place over the past few decades (*The Times*, 19 June 2000: 5; *Eleftherotypia*, 4 November 2003: 56; *Kyriakatiki Eleftherotypia*, 7 December 1997: 104–5). In the latter case, when there have been no incidents at all, or when such incidents are minor or infrequent, the press fuels insecurity by means of self-fulfilling prophecies. While journalists often resort to these (*La Repubblica*, 18 June 2000: 1; *The Times*, 19 June 2000: 4; *Le Monde*, 2–3 April 2006: 15), they try to boost the authority of what they write by citing police sources or quoting directly from representatives of the police or intelligence services. For example, during the 1998 World Cup, French intelligence officials said that they were expecting serious incidents between German and English football supporters in Lens (*Le Monde*, 25 June 1998: 1, 8); at the beginning of Euro 2000, it was reported that 'Belgian police fear that a pan-European racist alliance plans to provoke major unrest in Brussels' (*The Observer*, 11 June 2000: 5); before the 2002 World Cup, the head of specialist intelligence at the National Criminal Intelligence Service (NCIS) said that football hooligans might succeed in getting to the tournament because 'several bars in Thai resorts [were] owned by expatriate Britons with links to football hooliganism' (*Independent*, 18 May 2002: 4); and during the 2006 World Cup, a senior police source warned that 'German hooligans unite to target England fans' (*The Times*, 19 June 2006: 20).[6] When there are no incidents, the sense of threat is sustained indirectly. For example, at the time of the 2002 World Cup, in an article entitled 'Our gift to the Russians', a journalist explained at length how the football riots that broke out in Moscow during the tournament were 'inspired by British hooliganism' (*The Times*, 11 June 2002); in 2007, after England played Andorra, journalists expressed concern at the presence on the terraces of previously banned football hooligans who had served their suspensions and speculated on whether it might lead to a revival of football hooliganism (*The Times*, 30 March 2007: 117).

The amplification of the threat is also achieved by including many incidents in the same article, regardless of the danger they pose. The indiscriminate reporting of several incidents, ranging from the throwing of plastic glasses at a man of North African appearance to clashes involving large groups of people, conveys such a strong impression of wholesale trouble that the scene can then be plausibly described as 'chaotic' or 'multinational mayhem' (*The Observer*, 18 June 2000: 1). The insecurity thus created is further reinforced by means of a bipartite discursive mechanism that transforms probability into certainty and demolishes all dividing walls between the centre and periphery of the space occupied by the threat. Potential threats are therefore presented as highly probable, while isolated behaviours, situated at the periphery of the threat's space, are presented as mass collective behaviours that occupy, or might come to occupy, a central position within that space. So, despite the absence of any evidence of the existence of international networks of football hooligans, right from the start of Euro 2000 several journalists focused particular attention on the existence of an international, anti-Turkish hooligan alliance (*The Observer*, 11 June 2000: 5; *The Sunday Times*, 11 June 2000: 12).

Yet, in spite of this amplification of deviance, the social impact of the threat of football hooliganism remained limited because the threat itself did not extend beyond the sports context. Therefore, it was not possible to magnify its impact further unless it was presented as being potentially limitless. Football hooliganism thus became bound up with other criminal phenomena, to include urban riots, drug trafficking and even terrorism. While prior to the 1998 World Cup the French Interior Minister presented football hooliganism as being on a par with the threat to security posed by terrorism (*Le Figaro*, 23 June 1998: 38), subsequent evaluation of the event stressed that the tournament had 'also served as a pretext for urban violence' (*Le Monde*, 14 July 1998: xiii). The authorities also announced that the system of cooperation between police and judges used during the tournament was 'likely to be implemented on other occasions, particularly in the suburbs' (*Le Figaro*, 2 July 1998: 8C). Following the same reasoning, during Euro 2000, which was hosted by Belgium and the Netherlands, it was reported that 'several of the "generals" who organize football violence [were] involved in drug trafficking' and that the tournament was being used as 'a cover for drug smuggling' (*The Sunday Times*, 18 June 2000: 2). This information, which was based on a statement by a senior police officer, was presented in such a way that it was impossible to discern whether it was a widespread phenomenon or an isolated case. Similar question marks were raised by the headline 'Drugs fuel the mayhem'. While, logically speaking, it created the impression that mayhem was caused by drug users, in reality it referred to the fact that the 'police believe[d] the absence [of cannabis] may have contributed to the trouble' [in Belgium] since the secret of the successful control of English fans in the Netherlands 'lay in the coffee shops of Holland' (*The Sunday Times*, 18 June 2000: 2). This readiness to incorporate football hooliganism into a set of more serious criminal behaviours also underlay a statement made by an Italian police officer who, commenting on the ransacking of a police station by football supporters after one of their number was killed by the police, called their behaviour 'subversive violence' and an 'attack on [Italian] institutions' (*Corriere della Sera*, 24 November 2007: 10).

2   Security versus civil liberties

The need to improve control of this threat gave rise to a wave of calls from journalists, government and sport officials (*Independent*, 19 June 2000: 1; *Le Soir*, 20 June 2000: 2; *Libre Belgique*, 5 February 2007)[7] and even academics (I. Panoussis, in *Kathimerini*, 31 March 2007: 4; D. Bodin, in *Le Monde*, 1 March 2008: 27) for security measures to be stepped up, usually citing the British model as the example to follow (*Nea*, 18–19 November 2000: 59; *Le Monde*, 25 January 2003: 8; *La Stampa*, 17 April 2005: 24). It is noteworthy that, although most British scholars have attributed the decline in football-related disorder in Premier League stadia mainly to the vastly increased price of tickets and have pointed out that this policy has resulted in violence being displaced to lower division stadia and other non-sport-related areas (Redhead 1997: 24–5; Dunning 1999: 133, 2000: 147–50), public discourses in continental Europe have usually remained silent on the perverse effects of the implementation of the British counter-hooliganism model and tended to attribute its 'success' solely to the actions of law enforcers.

The impact of these calls for the enhancement of security measures was reinforced not only by the consensus that existed with regard to the seriousness of the threat but also by the increasing value placed on the oveall need to safeguard security. The importance attributed to security in journalistic circles was demonstrated by the frequent extensive coverage given to statements made by police and intelligence officers (*Libération*, 22 October 2002: 28–9; *Le Monde*, 25 January 2003: 8; *Corriere della Sera*, 26 March 2004: 10). Reflecting journalists' customary concern to support their articles with quotes from authoritative external sources (Neveu 2001/2004: 57ff; Koren 1996: 44ff), the words of law enforcers were from then on given more and more space, something which, of course, could not be dissociated from the EU Council's clear desire to improve cooperation between the police and the media by setting in place a media policy and communication strategy with regard to international fixtures and tournaments (Council of the EU 1997: 3, 1999: ch. 5, 2001: ch. 5, 2006c: ch. 5). Seen as experts, senior police and intelligence officers are now in a very powerful position vis-à-vis all the actors involved in the representation of football hooliganism. Consequently, not only are their statements given extensive press coverage, but the content of these is never called into question. As a result, football hooliganism tends to be seen through their eyes only.

The importance accorded to the value of security is also evident in the long, detailed descriptions in press articles of the security measures implemented at the time of high-risk matches and international tournaments. These tend to emphasize the technological progress made in that regard (electronic surveillance, the exchange of computerized data), the improvement of police strategies (coordination, planning, intelligence, spotters), the streamlining of the use of human resources (international police cooperation, the broadening of cooperation to include judges, travel agencies and airlines) and the implementation of new measures, such as the use of preventive detention and football bans. The purpose of conveying this image of well-equipped public security agencies, whose mission is highly streamlined and who work in close cooperation with each other as well as with civil society, is, above all, to reassure the populations concerned by confirming that the state apparatus within any given country is capable of effectively protecting people and property. Even when the effectiveness of that apparatus can reasonably be called into question, especially when such incidents occur, importance is placed on reporting anodyne statements made by those responsible for public security agencies or, if necessary, representatives of the political class. In contrast, with the exception of the Belgian press which frequently refers to *Fan Coaching*, the social prevention programmes established in some European countries as a 'soft' method of handling football hooliganism often receive no mention at all or, if they do, it is only to discredit them. Thus, during the 1998 World Cup, the French press only referred to the German *Fan Projekts* after serious incidents occurred in Lens specifically involving German football hooligans (*Le Figaro*, 23 June 1998: 38; *Libération*, 23 June 1998: 4).

The importance accorded to security is also clear both from the public approval given to the 'zero tolerance' policies adopted by foreign governments during international tournaments and from the tendency to dismiss the protests of football supporters in the event of unjustified repression. Thus, even when they emanated from reliable sources, complaints about the heavy-handed policing employed by the Belgian police during Euro 2000 were dismissed as 'rubbish' (*Independent*, 19 June 2000: 3)[8] and described as a 'snivelling whine about other people's policemen' (*Guardian*, 20 June 2000: 22).[9]

This widespread attitude is coupled with a tendency to discredit any pro-civil rights arguments. During Euro 2000, therefore, civil rights issues were in fact blamed for the incidents that broke out in Brussels and Charleroi. Contrasting the UK's refusal, on the grounds of protecting civil liberties, to pass a law allowing passports to be withdrawn from football supporters who had no criminal record of hooliganism with Germany's introduction of a law that prevented troublemakers from leaving the country, the Belgian press ironically commented that 'Nobody takes civil rights lightly in the country of habeas corpus: human rights' organizations went on the offensive and the law was never passed' (*Le Soir*, 20 June 2000: 4). While a British journalist said, 'It's no good talking about civil rights when genuine fans and the inhabitants of Charleroi and Brussels can't walk the streets in peace'

(*The Observer*, 18 June 2000: 3), the pro-civil rights stance taken by the British government was believed to be primarily due to 'administrative incompetence' since the same ministers had had no hesitation in passing the 1998 Terrorism and Conspiracy Bill, 'handing over the civil rights of suspect terrorists to the mere opinions of policemen and politicians about their guilt or innocence' (*Guardian*, 20 June 2000: 22). The latter constituted a new step in that it called into doubt the effectiveness of respect for civil rights and liberties in a society that is allegedly under threat from an increasing range of sources. If civil rights can be sacrificed in the name of fighting terrorism, why not also in the name of fighting football hooliganism? This discourse, which is entirely consistent with the dominant global threat perception, now refrains from categorizing the different threats according to their level of dangerousness while, at the same time, presenting civil rights as a major obstacle to the protection of internal security within the EU countries, thereby implicitly acknowledging that security takes precedence over fundamental freedoms.

Quite unsurprisingly then, no one has criticized the broad-ranging control of deviance that has been established as a result of the numerous counter-hooliganism surveillance and control measures currently in place and few have questioned the expulsion and detention of potential troublemakers from international tournaments. Direct challenges to the validity of the coercive measures taken against those who are simply suspected of involvement in football hooliganism (*Le Monde*, 23 June 1998: II) and statements in their defence, such as 'We cannot deny people the protection of our principles because they do not happen to be our cup of tea' (*Independent*, 5 June 2002: 17), remain rare although they have occasionally been backed up by assertions from jurists that security measures have been implemented at the expense of football supporters' human rights (I. Blackshaw, in *The Times*, 28 May 2002).[10] This marginalization of any criticism of security measures has not really been balanced by the occasional reporting of the views of football supporters because, since they tend to be portrayed as the only ones alleging that their rights have been violated (*Le Monde*, 17 March 2006: 16), they are ultimately indirectly discredited, precisely because their allegations are not backed by others.

Although, at first sight, media coverage of the phenomenon is the most visible part of the process through which football hooliganism is defined and the security measures used to deal with it are legitimated, it is worth remembering that the media do not act alone. It is not a matter of measuring the impact of one type of media discourse or another on the formation of public opinion. Nor is it a matter of measuring its possible effects on the political field. The representation of football hooliganism I have examined in this book has been constructed gradually, over four decades, in accordance with the socio-political evolution of each of the societies concerned rather than the evolution of the phenomenon itself, and would never have achieved dominance on a European scale if it had not been based on the conceptual axes which have determined development of the political and security fields in the post-Cold War era. At the same time, these new concepts and their translation into law and security practices could not have been effectively spread and legitimated without the compliance of the media, among others. In the absence of both significant counter-arguments, especially from academia, and a legal definition of the phenomenon, the dynamic unleashed by the interactions that have taken place within this circular process has, thanks to its perseverance, ended up establishing its master plan everywhere as evidence. Given this state of affairs, the breaching of civil liberties has become invisible to society because legal abnormality is now accepted as normal.

Notes

Introduction

1. European level refers to decisions taken by either the Council of Europe or the Union of European Football Associations (UEFA).
2. Due to the use of knives and other weapons.
3. Although such violence occurs mainly at football matches, in several European countries it can also be found at basketball, volleyball, ice-hockey and water-polo matches.
4. On 29 May 1985, about one hour before the kick-off of the European Cup Final between Liverpool and Juventus, a group of English fans charged towards Italian supporters. While seeking to retreat, the latter put pressure on a dilapidated wall, which collapsed on top of them, leaving 39 fans dead and more than 600 injured.
5. This controversy, which flared up following the publication in 1991 of a special issue of *The Sociological Review*, raged throughout the 1990s and still affects the debate to this day.
6. Belgium, France, Greece, Italy, the Netherlands and the UK.
7. Belgium, France, Greece, Italy and the UK.
8. For example, the countries of Scandinavia.
9. In the event that an author's work covers more than one period, he is mentioned in the period during which most work was produced.

Introduction to Part I

1. Football hooliganism emerged in Italy, Belgium and the Netherlands in the early 1970s. By the end of the 1970s, it was also to be found in Germany, Greece and Spain.
2. This statement is not unproblematic. In fact, there is no way to define clearly what constitutes a 'football-related incident'. Official statistics are often biased and in many countries vary considerably from one institution to another. Press coverage is unreliable; individual perceptions differ. Moreover, it is not easy to distinguish 'minor' football-related incidents from 'serious' ones. Nor is it possible to use the number of arrests as a reliable gauge because the figures can vary greatly depending on domestic, and even case-specific, law enforcement policies and practices. If one takes the number of people injured and/or the cost of material damage to be a more reliable gauge, then the incidents involving English football supporters during Euro 2000 were definitely minor. Yet they were presented as being serious enough to justify the introduction of more repressive legislation in the UK. On the other hand, the 2006 World Cup was presented as being an 'incident-free' tournament despite the fact that in their final statement the German authorities announced that there had been around 9,000 arrests in the course of the event. If, however, human

casualties and material damage are combined with other, more biased criteria (the frequency of reported incidents, the number of arrests, data from various official statistics, and so on) they do suggest that football hooliganism was on the rise during the 1970s and 1980s. The increasing seriousness of football-related incidents at international matches was demonstrated by, for example, the football riots that occurred in May 1974 during the Feyenoord–Tottenham match (where hundreds were injured) and those that broke out in September 1980 during the Castilla–West Ham match (where one person died). At the domestic level, rioting took place in January 1980 at the Swansea–Crystal Palace match (UK), resulting in the death of one supporter, in June 1981 at the Campobasso–Tirenni match (Italy) and in May 1982 at the Bayern–Nuremberg match (Germany), where over 100 were injured, while in April 1982, during the AZ Alkmaar 67–Feyenoord match (Netherlands), an explosive device was thrown on the pitch by a supporter.

1   Early academic theories

1. This term applies to any act of ritualized aggression effected at the symbolic level in accordance with a set of rules established, often implicitly, by each group of football hooligans.
2. Conceived as forming homocentric circles, these stages defined the status of football hooligans within their group; those concerned could only move on from one stage to another after successfully undergoing certain initiation rites.
3. In the 1990s, Scottish researchers nevertheless showed that relations between the early football supporters' groups and officials at Scottish football clubs were much closer and open than in England, revealing the existence of a kind of participatory democracy similar to that described by Taylor, without, however, linking its disappearance to football hooliganism (Moorhouse 1994: 175–7, quoted by Taylor 2006: 102).
4. In the aftermath of the Heysel tragedy, English football clubs were banned from all European competitions by UEFA. The ban was lifted after five years.

2   A non-specific legal framework

1. See Introduction to Part I, note 1 above.
2. In the UK, for instance, the first official report on football hooliganism (the Lang Report) was published in 1969 and the second (*Football Spectator Violence*) in 1984.

3   Divergent policing styles

1. In the UK, electronic surveillance has been used in football stadia since the early 1970s (Taylor 1982a: 46; Armstrong and Giulianotti 1998: 121).
2. Inside grounds, segregation was ensured, on the one hand, through a policy of controlling the sale of match tickets and, on the other, by means of a human wall of police officers or various types of physical barrier (railings,

wire fencing, and so on) placed between the different sets of supporters as well as between the terraces and the pitch. Outside the grounds, segregation was ensured mainly by having a police presence along the route taken by the away team supporters to get to the stadium and by providing them with a police escort from their place of arrival in the town or city in question to the stadium and from the stadium to their place of departure.

3. Largely the desire of the Ministry of Sport, this initiative was taken following the success of the United Kingdom Football Liaison Group during the 1982 World Cup. The purpose of the network, which entered into operation in 1981 under the auspices of the Ministry of Sport, was to advise the football club managements and public authorities concerned whenever an English football club was participating in a European tournament.

4   The social construction of 'otherness'

1. My analysis encompasses the following newspapers: *Le Monde, Libération, Le Figaro, Le Journal du Dimanche* (France); *La Stampa, Corriere della Sera, La Repubblica* (Italy); *The Times, Guardian, The Observer* (UK).

2. For practical reasons, the presentation of each point relies on a selection of quotations that are believed to be representative of its whole coverage. When, for technical reasons, the specific page numbers are not available, I cite the headline.

3. Though frequently observed, mutual reinforcement of public discourses and policies is not a necessary condition for successfully implementing public policies. For an analysis of a case in which public discourses and policies diverged, see Tsoukala (2008b).

4. 'Soccer marches to war'; 'Soccer is sick at the moment. Or, better, its crowds seem to have contracted some disease that causes them to break out in fury' (*Sun*, 8 November 1965, quoted by Dunning et al., 1988: 150).

5. Quoted by Whannel 1979: 331.

6. Quoted by Wagg 1984: 212.

7. Statement by the Home Secretary.

8. Statement by the Home Secretary.

9. Quoted by Taylor 1982a: 52.

10. Quoted by Weir 1980: 319.

Introduction to Part II

1. An influence attested to not only by the references made to the British works, which were much more numerous than the references made to other European works by British researchers, but also by the whole range of papers published in that period. In fact, apart from one Italian book, all the collective volumes published at that time which addressed the issue in several different countries were edited by British scholars.

2. An argument often used by many of the security professionals I interviewed.

3. This does not mean that academia should be actively involved in policy-making. Given the risk that, by doing so, scholars could easily be turned into the unwitting legitimators of social control policies, if not law enforcement

'auxiliaries', whether or not to participate in policy-making and, if so, to what extent and at what level is a highly subjective matter and as such is neither defended nor discussed here. What is at stake is academia's authority as a key definer of social problems and its ensuing ability to impose its definitions within the public sphere.

5   The vibrancy of the academic community

1. Such as sports fanaticism, the sporting significance and ups and downs of matches, flawed policing and the fact that leaders of the group may have incited others to take action.
2. The English model refers to loosely organized football supporters' groups who show their support in the stadium by singing together. With violence being an integral part of their behaviour, the young men involved in football-related incidents can always count on the solidarity of other supporters, who will not hesitate to go to their aid if necessary. The Italian model refers to extremely well-organized football supporters' groups who express their support in the stadium by putting on proper shows on the terraces (smoke grenades, flags, firecrackers, choreographed movements, and so on). Although regularly involved in violence, they do not accord it the same level of importance as their counterparts in Northern Europe do.
3. The notion of militancy is currently being used more and more frequently to describe the milieu of the football supporter without, however, subjecting it to any type of theoretical analysis. See, for instance, Mignon 1998: 231ff; Hourcade 2000: 124; Le Noé 1998: 59.
4. For an in-depth study of this thesis, see the many articles that appeared between 1975 and 1997 in the journal *Quel corps?*
5. A term borrowed from the work of Norbert Elias.
6. In particular, hostility to the school system, a strong sense of territorial identification and hostility to anyone from outside.
7. Among the few studies that analyse football hooliganism in terms of sexual behaviour, see Bairner 1999; Free and Hughson 2003.
8. In *Causes of Delinquency*, T. Hirschi looks at the impact weak or strong social bonds have on the decision whether or not to engage in crime. In this respect, he distinguishes four elements: attachment to parents, peers or school; commitment to conventional lines of action; involvement in conventional activities; and belief in a common value.

6   Paradoxical legal specificity

1. This was the first time that international cooperation had been properly regulated.
2. For example, consumption of alcohol in and around football stadia, and, in some countries, possession of intoxicating liquor while travelling to or from a designated sporting event.
3. Introduced throughout this period as well as during the subsequent one.
4. Mainly introduced during the subsequent period.

5. This was well illustrated by the titles given to the regulatory texts adopted on the subject both at the European level and in many European countries, which invariably mentioned this spatial element.

6. This is a paraphrase of a comment made by Blakesley 1998: 41 when seeking to define organized crime.

7. These would include bodily harm and damage to property.

8. These types of acts would include repeatedly standing up and/or shouting abuse (inside stadia), drinking alcohol or being part of a rowdy group (outside stadia).

9. One of the best illustrations comes from the Netherlands where, in the mid-2000s, spotters visited potential troublemakers in their homes to warn them that they needed to change their behaviour if they wished to avoid arrest.

10. In Spain, for example, this type of behaviour was made an offence under Law No. 10/1990; in the UK, the first special law that made it an offence was the Football (Offences) Act 1991; in Greece, racist incidents involving football supporters continued to be dealt with solely under general legislation throughout this period.

11. Features which had been weakened included the ability to legislate and the decision-making process with regard to economic and financial affairs, social affairs, and so on; features which had disappeared included the removal of internal border controls by the signatories of the Schengen Agreement and the abolition of national currencies in the states within the Eurozone.

12. Rigakos and Hadden 2001 call into question the idea that the risk society is a product of late modernity. Instead they link it to the aims and interests of incipient seventeenth-century English capitalism. I believe, however, that even if the actuarial risk management approach does date back to the seventeenth century, an important turning point has occurred over the past few decades in that, for the first time in history, risk management has become widely accepted and even institutionalized in all European countries as the most appropriate method of crime control.

13. Sport was first mentioned in a declaration appended to the Treaty of Amsterdam that had no binding effect. It only became an EU policy area in the Treaty of Lisbon.

14. As sport was not a Community objective, the European Community bodies were unable to legislate on football hooliganism. During this period, their initiatives were confined to the following: a) the Adonnino Report, adopted by the Milan European Council in June 1985, which recommended the reinforcement of preventive and coercive measures for dealing with football hooliganism (Resolution of 13 November 1985, Europe of the citizens, OJEC C345, 31 December 1985); b) a request made to the K4 Commission by the JHA Council, during its meeting on 20 and 21 June 1995, asking it to submit proposals to it on improving measures for dealing with football hooliganism.

15. While the authors of the 1985 European Convention admitted that the origins of football spectator violence were mainly outside sport, the only long-term preventive policy they proposed was sports-focused, that is, it relied primarily on the promotion of the sporting ideal and the notion of fair play. Moreover, in its first annual report, the Standing Committee considered that research into the social origins of football hooliganism would not

be directly helpful in implementing the European Convention (First meeting of the Standing Committee, Meeting Report 4, 8–9 July 1986, quoted by Taylor (1987: 638).

7   Convergent policing styles

1. This gradual change did not mean that the repressive styles of policing that prevailed in the past completely disappeared. Several scholars have pointed out that they are still in use in Italy, for instance (Marchi 2005; Louis 2006: 109ff).
2. The tightening of police control made bare-knuckle fighting less popular since, precisely because it went on for longer, it increased the chances of arrest for those involved. The risk of being arrested was therefore often minimized by the use of weapons which allowed the same, if not better, result to be obtained in less time.
3. Except for a short period in a few places in Italy (De Biasi 1998).
4. Germany, Belgium and the Netherlands.
5. In the UK, where this measure was most widely implemented, undercover policing of football supporters' groups had been recommended by the Football Association as far back as the 1960s, but was only carried out on a large scale after 1985. Other European countries still have reservations about this rather sensitive issue but the German police did, for example, announce that they were going to infiltrate football supporters' groups in order to enhance security during the 2006 World Cup.
6. In 1992, it succeeded the National Football Intelligence Unit which had been set up in 1989.
7. Of the 6,000 individuals recorded in the database in 1992, over 4,000 were there for having committed non-violent offences in a sporting context (using drugs, selling match tickets on the black market, and so on) or for having been seen in the company of football hooligans (Armstrong and Hobbs 1994: 222).
8. This was hastened by the Single European Act 1986, which proclaimed freedom of movement within the European Community.
9. Brought in as a result of the Sporting Events (Control of Alcohol etc.) Act 1985, these measures soon prompted reservations as to their suitability (Greenfield and Osborn 2001: 34–5).
10. Such as the installation of CCTV in stadia and rules on the setting up of football supporters' clubs.
11. To this day, the event at which the failure of security services to collaborate with each other had the most disastrous consequences was the Heysel Stadium tragedy in 1985 (Tulkens 1988; Govaert and Comeron 1995).
12. A failure that was illustrated throughout the 1970s and in the first half of the 1980s by the increased frequency and seriousness of violent incidents involving English football supporters both inside the country and abroad.
13. These included, for example, Greece and Austria, which long resisted the setting up of information centres, and the Netherlands, which was still reluctant to include potential troublemakers in the CIV files and pass on the names of such individuals to their foreign counterparts.

14. One of the clearest examples of this was the call made by the public security agencies in the Netherlands (National Consultative Committee on Football Hooliganism 1987).
15. Public security agencies were often accused of having contributed to the outbreak and/or escalation of football-related incidents because of their lax attitude or inappropriate interventions.
16. That was the case, for instance, in the UK and the Netherlands.
17. That was the case, for instance, in Italy and Greece.
18. For example, when they were looking for work and/or accommodation or applying for social benefits.
19. This consisted mainly of vocational guidance for young people or legal advice if they had been arrested.
20. By helping them, for example, to organize their travel to away matches or publish their fanzines.
21. The clubs received funding for this from the *Deutscher Fussball-Bund.*
22. Professor Georges Kellens (University of Liège) and Professor Lode Walgrave (Catholic University of Leuven).
23. This view was broadly shared by all the Belgian security professionals I interviewed in 2007.
24. It was not a question of passing on details about named individuals but solely information of a general nature that might improve the management of security.

8 The general acceptance of 'otherness'

1. The chain of responsibility established by the Belgian courts included sports officials and local authorities, as well as representatives of the police and gendarmerie.
2. My analysis encompasses the following national newspapers: *Le Monde, Libération, Le Figaro, Le Journal du Dimanche* (France); *La Stampa, Corriere della Sera, La Repubblica* (Italy); *The Times, The Sunday Times, Guardian, Independent, The Observer* (UK); *I Kathimerini, Ta Nea, Eleftherotypia, Kyriakatiki Eleftherotypia, To Vima* (Greece).
3. 'The Return to Europe – Monihan Reverses Charge'.
4. Statement by the Prime Minister.
5. Statement by a Conservative MP.
6. I was present at the Symposium.
7. 'Howell Sick as a Parrot, but Minister over the Cameroon'.
8. In-depth analysis is rare but not totally nonexistent. See, for instance, J. Seabrook, 'The Seeds of Violence' (*Guardian*, 3 June 1985: 9); 'We Were Like Animals in a Zoo' (*Guardian*, 17 April 1989: 19).
9. Statement by Mr Justice Popplewell.
10. Statement by the Prime Minister.
11. Quoted by Murphy et al. 1990: 184.
12. While admitting that the police in the host country had good reason to want to minimize the extent of any possible incidents, there was a considerable gulf between the media coverage of the rioting in Stockholm during the 1992 European Championship and the following statement made by a Swedish

senior police officer, 'The damage was no more than for a normal Friday or Saturday night' ('Germans Take up Hooligan Mantle', *The Times*, 19 June 1992).

13. Statement by Malcolm George, Greater Manchester's Assistant Chief Constable.

14. A rare example of criticism, which appeared in *The Times*, 22 June 1990, under the headline 'Hooligan Treatment May Be in Breach of EC Law', concerned the expulsion by the Italian authorities of English football supporters who were viewed as dangerous by the British intelligence services. Picking up on an article which appeared in the *Solicitor's Journal*, it said that 'blanket bans, decisions based on lists compiled of "undesirable aliens" without further individual information or without serious misconduct in Italy are forbidden under Community law. Restrictions imposed by a Member State on EC nationals moving from one Community state to another can be imposed only in exceptional circumstances and based on proven conduct of individuals'. On the other hand, the security measures taken abroad were not above criticism. For example, the heavy and indiscriminate policing during the 1990 World Cup in Italy was the subject of several press articles (see articles in *Guardian* of 28 June, 3, 7 July 1990, and *Independent* of 18 June, 3 July 1990).

15. Statements by Swedish police officers.

16. Such as slaves, black people or the indigenous peoples of Latin America.

17. Statement by a basketball champion.

18. Interviewed by the author in 1996.

19. 'The Official Cloak of Football Hooliganism'.

10   Legal vagueness

1. In the Council Resolution of 29 April 2004, the definition of the target population was changed to cover individuals or groups in respect of whom there are substantial grounds for believing that they intend to enter the Member State with the aim of disrupting public order and security at the event or committing offences relating to the event (art. 1).

2. The operational details of this cooperation were specified in the Council Resolution of 21 June 1999. That Council Resolution was later updated and expanded by the Council Resolution of 6 December 2001.

3. Although these conclusions have no binding effect, Member States are expected to abide by them.

4. The note (7386/98 ENFOPOL 45) was sent from the Presidency of the Council to a Cooperation Group of experts on public order to prepare an experts meeting on public order and conflict management to be held in Brussels on 15 April 1998 (Statewatch 1998).

5. During this period, the Council of Europe's policy was evident mainly in the Recommendations regularly adopted by the Standing Committee of the 1985 European Convention.

6. Law No. 401 of 13 December 1989 (Art. 6), *Gazzetta Ufficiale* No. 294, 18 December 1989.
7. In Greece, for instance, they were introduced in 1986 by Law 1646 on preventive and coercive measures against violence in sport, *FEK*, 18 September 1986, A 138.
8. In Belgium, for example, they were introduced in 1998 by the Law on security at football matches, *Moniteur belge*, 3 February 1999 (as amended by the Law of 10 March 2003, *Moniteur belge*, 31 March 2003, and the Law of 25 April 2007, *Moniteur belge*, 8 May 2007).
9. For a period of 3–10 years.
10. For a period of 3–5 years.
11. A statement must first be taken from the offender; the police officer must inform him that he is being subjected to a banning order and must make a written report of the facts including specific details, which must be certified by an official.
12. Laws LJ in *Gough vs Chief Constable of Derbyshire* (2001) QBD, §45. The ruling was endorsed by the Court of Appeal in *Gough vs Chief Constable of Derbyshire*, 20 March 2002, §89.
13. The Council considers the reintroduction of border controls necessary not only in the context of tournaments but also in the context of high-risk international matches (Council of the EU 2001b: II-c).

11   The decompartmentalization of policing

1. I am thinking in particular of spatial criteria (that differentiate, for example, threats located inside a country from those located outside its borders, and threats at local level from those at national level) and the criteria used to rank threats according to their level of dangerousness, ranging from petty crime to organized crime and terrorism.
2. This proposal was put forward when Belgium held the EU presidency, following an experts meeting on football hooliganism, held in Brussels (22–23 May 2001).
3. Namely, the Scandinavian countries, with Austria and Greece.
4. This provision is repeated in the Council Resolution of 17 November 2003: art. 6.
5. This is the Police Cooperation Working Party. The operational framework of this group, which has to work closely with both the Council of Europe and UEFA, was set out by the Council of the EU (2007b).
6. In the Netherlands, during Euro 2000, and in Portugal, during Euro 2004.
7. This was the initiative known as Kick It! (www.kickit-berlin.de).
8. It was mentioned in particular in Greece (*Eleftherotypia*, 21 June 2006) and Hungary (*Magyar hirlap*, 6 June 2006).
9. See, for instance, the UEFA's binding instructions (2004: point 4).
10. The first Fans Embassy was organized during the 1990 World Cup in Italy.
11. Visits to schools, friendly football matches, the clearing of litter from beaches, etc.

12   The consensus around security

1. My analysis encompasses the following national newspapers: *The Times, The Sunday Times, Guardian, The Observer, Independent* (UK); *Le Monde, Libération, Le Figaro, Le Journal du Dimanche* (France); *Eleftherotypia, Kyriakatiki Eleftherotypia, I Kathimerini, Ta Nea, To Vima* (Greece); *La Repubblica, La Stampa, Corriere della Sera* (Italy); *Le Soir, La Libre Belgique* (Belgium).
2. 'Un nouveau projet de loi contre la violence'.
3. 'Le hooliganisme? La bête n'est pas morte'.
4. 'Ex-fan des eighties Dougie n'est plus hooligan'.
5. On the powerlessness of English football supporters in the face of this dominant discourse, see Perryman (2006).
6. Concern about the possibility of violent incidents involving German and English football supporters was expressed well before the tournament began (*The Times*, 9 March 2006: 6).
7. 'Le hooliganisme? La bête n'est pas morte'.
8. Statement by a spokesman for the NCIS.
9. Statement by a senior police officer.
10. 'Even the football supporter has rights'.

References

Adang, O. and Cuvelier, C. *Policing Euro 2000* (Beek-Ubbergen: Tandem Felix; 2001).

Agamben, G. *Homo sacer* (Paris: Seuil, 1997).

Agamben, G. *Moyens sans fins* (Paris: Payot & Rivages, 2002).

Agozino, B. 'Changes in the Social Construct of Criminality among Immigrants in the United Kingdom', in S. Palidda (ed.), *Immigrant Delinquency* (Brussels: European Commission, 1997), pp. 103–31.

Alabarces, P., Tomlinson, A. and Young, C. 'Argentina versus England at the France '98 World Cup: Narratives of nation and the mythologizing of the popular', *Media, Culture & Society* 23(5) (2001) 547–66.

Albrecht, H.–J. 'La criminalité organisée et la notion de l'ordre', in Institut de Sciences Pénales et de Criminologie, *Criminalité organisée et ordre dans la société* (Marseille: Presses Universitaires d'Aix, 1997), pp. 17–27.

Altheide, D. L. *Terrorism and the Politics of Fear* (Lanham, MD: AltaMira Press, 2006).

Anderson, M. *Frontiers: Territory and State Formation in the Modern World* (Cambridge: Polity, 1996).

Anderson, M. and Boer, M. den (eds) *Policing across National Boundaries* (London: Pinter, 1994).

Anderson, M., Boer, M. den, Cullen, G. et al. *Policing the European Union* (Oxford: Clarendon Press, 1996).

Armstrong, G. 'False Leeds: the construction of hooligan confrontations', in R. Giulianotti and Williams J. (eds), *Game without Frontiers* (Aldershot: Arena, 1994), pp. 299–325.

Armstrong, G. *Football Hooligans* (Oxford: Berg, 1998).

Armstrong, G. and Giulianotti, R. 'From Another Angle: Police surveillance and football supporters', in C. Norris, J. Moran and G. Armstrong (eds), *Surveillance, Closed Circuit Television and Social Control* (Aldershot: Ashgate, 1998), pp. 113–35.

Armstrong, G. and Harris, R. 'Football Hooligans: Theory and evidence', *The Sociological Review* 39(3) (1991) 427–56.

Armstrong, G. and Hobbs, D. 'Tackled from Behind', in R. Giulianotti, N. Bonney and M. Hepworth (eds), *Football, Violence and Social Identity* (London: Routledge, 1994), pp. 196–228.

Armstrong, G. and Young, M. 'Legislators and Interpreters: the law and football hooligans', in G. Armstrong and R. Giulianotti (eds), *Entering the Field* (Oxford: Berg, 1997), pp. 175–91.

Assemblée Nationale (France) Rapport No. 396 sur la mise en application de la loi n° 2006–784 du 5 juillet 2006 relative à la prévention des violences lors des manifestations sportives, 7 November 2007.

Astrinakis, A. 'Subcultures of Hard-core Fans in West Attica: an analysis of some central research findings', in E. Dunning, P. Murphy, I. Waddington et al. (eds), *Fighting Fans* (Dublin: University College Dublin Press, 2002), pp. 88–105.

Astrinakis, A. and Stilianoudi, L. (eds) *Heavy Metal, Rockabili, Fanatikoi Opadoi* (Athens: Hellinika Grammata, 1996).

Augé, M. 'Football: de l'histoire sociale à l'anthropologie religieuse', *Le Débat* no. 19 (1982) 59–67.

Bairner, A. 'Soccer, Masculinity, and Violence in Northern Ireland', *Men and Masculinities* 1(3) (1999) 284–301.

Bairner, A. 'The Dog that Didn't Bark? Football hooliganism in Ireland', in E. Dunning, P. Murphy, I. Waddington et al. (eds), *Fighting Fans* (Dublin: University College Dublin Press, 2002), pp. 118–30.

Bairner, A. and Shirlow, P. 'Real and Imagined: Reflections on Football Rivalry in Northern Ireland', in G. Armstrong and R. Giulianotti (eds), *Fear and Loathing in World Football* (Oxford: Berg, 2001), pp. 43–60.

Baldaccini, A. and Guild, E. *Terrorism and the Foreigner* (The Hague: Martinus Nijhoff, 2006).

Balestri, C. and Viganò G. 'Gli ultra: origini, storia e sviluppi recenti di un mondo ribelle', *Quaderni di sociologia* XLVIII, no. 34 (2004) 37–49.

Ball-Rokeach, S. 'Values and Violence: a test of the subculture of violence thesis', *American Sociological Review* 38 (1973) 736–49.

Balzacq, T. and Carrera, S. (eds) *Security versus Freedom* (Aldershot: Ashgate, 2006).

Basson, J.-C. 'Les politiques de lutte contre le hooliganisme. Vers un référentiel européen d'action publique', in S. Roché (ed.), *Réformer la police et la sécurité* (Paris: Odile Jacob, 2004), pp. 313–30.

Bastit, M. *Naissance de la loi moderne* (Paris: PUF, 1990).

Bauman, Z. *Liquid Times* (Cambridge: Polity, 2007).

Bayley, D. H. *Patterns of Policing* (New Brunswick: Rutgers University Press, 1985).

Bayley, D. H. and Shearing, C. 'The Future of Policing', *Law and Society Review* 30, 3 (1996) 585–606.

Beck, U. *Risk Society* (London: Sage, 1992).

Beck, U. *World Risk Society* (Cambridge: Polity, 1999).

Beck, U. 'The Terrorist Threat. World risk society revisited', *Theory, Culture & Society* 19(4) (2002) 39–55.

Becker, H. *Outsiders* (New York: Free Press, 1963).

Beiu, A. 'Football Related Violence in Romania', X International Congress of History of Sport, *Sport and Violence*, Seville, 2–5 November 2005.

Berger, G. *Violence and Sports* (London: Watts, 1990).

Berkowitz, L. *Aggression* (New York: McGraw-Hill, 1962).

Bigo, D. *L'Europe des polices et de la sécurité intérieure* (Brussels: Complexe, 1992).

Bigo, D. 'The European Internal Security Field: Stakes and rivalries in a newly developing area of police intervention', in M. Anderson and M. den Boer (eds), *Policing across National Boundaries* (London: Pinter, 1994), pp. 161–73.

Bigo, D. *Polices en réseaux* (Paris: Presses de Sciences-Po, 1996).

Bigo, D. 'Le champ européen de la sécurité', in D. Bigo, J.-P. Hanon and A. Tsoukala, *Approche comparative des problèmes de sécurité intérieure*, Final Report (Paris: Ministry of Defence, 1999).

Bigo, D. 'When Two Becomes One: Internal and external securitizations in Europe', in M. Kelstrup and M. C. Williams (eds), *International Relations Theory and the Politics of European Integration* (London: Routledge, 2000), pp. 171–205.

Bigo, D. 'The Moebius Ribbon of Internal and External Security', in M. Albert, D. Yacobson and Y. Lapid (eds), *Identities, Borders, Orders* (Minneapolis: University of Minnesota Press, 2001), pp. 91–116.

Bigo, D. 'Security and Immigration: Toward a critique of the governmentality of unease', *Alternatives* 27, supplement (2002) 63–92.

Bigo, D. 'Les nouvelles formes de la gouvernementalité: surveiller et contrôler à distance', in M. C. Ganjon (ed.), *Penser avec Foucault* (Paris: Karthala, 2004), pp. 129–61.

Bigo, D. 'Exception et ban: à propos de "l'état d'exception"', *Erytheis* 2 (2007) <http://idt.uab.cat/erytheis>.

Bigo, D. 'Globalized (in)Security: the Field and the Ban-opticon', in D. Bigo and A. Tsoukala (eds), *Terror, Insecurity and Liberty* (London: Routledge, 2008), pp. 10–48.

Bishop, H. and Jaworski, A. 'We Beat 'em: Nationalism and the hegemony of homogeneity in the British press reportage of Germany versus England during Euro 2000', *Discourse & Society* 14(3) (2003) 243–71.

Blackshaw, I. 'The "English Disease" – Tackling Football Hooliganism in England', *International Sports Law Journal*, no.1–2 (2005) 90–1.

Blakesley, C. 'Les systèmes de justice criminelle face au défi du crime organisé', *Revue Internationale de Droit Pénal* 1/2 trimestres (1998) 35–68.

Bodin, D. *Hooliganisme, vérités et mensonges* (Paris: ESF, 1999).

Bodin, D. 'La déculturation du public du football comme facteur du hooliganisme. Mythe ou réalité?', *STAPS* no. 57 (2002) 85–106.

Bodin, D. Editorial, *International Review on Sport and Violence* 1 (2008) <http://www.irsv.org>.

Bodin, D., Héas, S. and Robène, L. 'Hooliganisme: de la question de l'anomie sociale et du déterminisme', *Champ pénal* 1 (2004a) <http://champpenal.revues.org>.

Bodin, D., Robène, L. and Héas, S. *Sports et violences en Europe* (Strasbourg: Council of Europe, 2004b).

Bodin, D. and Trouilhet, D. 'Le contrôle social des foules sportives en France: réglementation, difficultés d'application et extension des phénomènes de violences', in D. Bodin (ed.), *Sports et violences* (Paris: Chiron, 2002), pp. 147–68.

Bonditti, P. 'From Territorial Space to Networks: A Foucaldian approach to the implementation of biometry', *Alternatives* 29(4) (2004) 465–82.

Bonelli, L. 'Evolutions et régulations des illégalismes populaires en France depuis le début des années 1980', *Cultures & Conflits* no. 51 (2003) 9–42.

Bonelli, L. 'Policing the Youth: Towards a redefinition of discipline and social control in French working-class neighbourhoods', in S. Venkatesh and R. Kassimir (eds), *Youth, Globalization and the Law* (Chicago: Stanford University Press, 2007), pp. 90–123.

Bonelli, L. *La France a peur* (Paris: La Découverte, 2008).

Boniface, P. (ed.) *Géopolitique du football* (Brussels: Complexe, 1998).

Boniface, P. *La terre est ronde comme un ballon* (Paris: Seuil, 2002).

Borghini, F. *Violenza negli stadi* (Florence: Manzuoli Luciano, 1977).

Boudon, R. *Effet pervers et ordre social* (Paris: PUF, 1977).

Boudon, R. *La logique du social* (Paris: Hachette, 1979).

Boyle, R. 'A Small Country with a Big Ambition. Representations of Portugal and England in Euro 2004 British and Portuguese newspaper coverage', *European Journal of Communication* 20(2) (2005) 223–44.

Brimson, D. *Eurotrashed* (London: Headline, 2003).

Brohm, J.–M. 'La religion sportive. Eléments d'analyse des faits religieux dans la pratique sportive', *Actions et Recherches Sociales* 10–13(3) (1983) 101–17.

Brohm, J.–M. *Les meutes sportives* (Paris: L'Harmattan, 1993).

Brohm, J.–M. *Les shootés du stade* (Paris: Paris-Méditerranée, 1998).

Brohm, J.–M. *La machinerie sportive* (Paris: Anthropos, 2002).

Brohm, J.-M. and Perelman, M. *Le football, une peste émotionnelle* (Paris: Gallimard, 2006).

Bromberger, C. 'L'Olympique de Marseille, la Juve et le Torino', *Esprit* no. 4 (1984) 174–95.

Bromberger, C. 'La passion partisane chez les ultra', *Les Cahiers de la sécurité intérieure* no. 26 (1996) 33–6.

Bromberger, C. *Le match de football* (Paris: Maison des sciences de l'homme, 1998).

Bromberger, C., Hayot, A. and Mariottini, J. M. 'Allez l'OM! Forza Juve! La passion pour le football à Marseille et à Turin', *Terrain* no. 8 (1987) 8–41.

Broussard, P. *Génération supporter* (Paris: Robert Laffont, 1990).

Broussard, P. 'La sécurité reste le premier enjeu de l'Euro 2000', *Le Monde* (8 June 2000) 28.

Brouwer, E., Catz, P. and Guild, E. *Immigration, Asylum and Terrorism* (Nijmegen: Instituut voor Rechtssociologie, 2003).

Brug, H. van der 'Il teppismo calcistico in Olanda', in A. Roversi (ed.), *Calcio e violenza in Europa* (Bologna: Il Mulino, 1990) pp. 107–37.

Brug, H. van der 'Football hooliganism in the Netherlands', in R. Giulianotti, N. Bonney and M. Hepworth (eds), *Football, Violence and Social Identity* (London: Routledge, 1994) pp. 174–95.

Burgat, F. 'La logique de la légitimation de la violence: animalité vs humanité', in F. Héritier (ed.), *De la violence II* (Paris: Odile Jacob, 1999) pp. 44–62.

Busset, T. 'Le supportérisme violent en Suisse: un état des lieux', *Revue internationale de criminologie et de police technique et scientifique* LV (2002) 348–57.

Buzan, B., Waever, O. and Wilde, J. D. *Security: A New Framework for Analysis* (Boulder, CO: Lynne Riener, 1998).

Campbell, B. and Dawson, A. 'Indecent Exposures, Men, Masculinity and Violence', in M. Perryman (ed.), *Hooligan Wars* (Edinburgh: Mainstream Publishing, 2002), pp. 62–76.

Cappelle, J. 'La police et la contestation publique en Grande-Bretagne 1980–1987', *Déviance et Société* 13(1) (1989) 35–79.

Castel, R. *L'insécurité sociale* (Paris: Seuil, 2003).

Ceyhan, A. 'Technologie et sécurité: une gouvernance libérale dans un contexte d'incertitudes', *Cultures & Conflits* no. 64 (2007) 11–32.

Ceyhan, A. and Tsoukala, A. 'The Securitization of Migration in Western Societies: Ambivalent discourses and practices', *Alternatives* 27, supplement (2002) 21–39.

Champagne, P. 'La construction médiatique des malaises sociaux', *Actes de la recherche en sciences sociales* no. 90 (1991) 64–75.

Chaplin, M. 'UEFA Addresses Violence' (28 November 2007) <http://www.uefa.com>.

Chaplin, M. 'L'UEFA lance sa campagne Respect' (12 March 2008) <http://fr.euro2008.uefa.com>.

Chatard, R. *La violence des spectateurs dans le football européen* (Paris: Lavauzelle, 1994).

Chevalier, L. *Classes laborieuses et classes dangereuses à Paris pendant la première moitié du XIXe siècle* (Paris: Plon, 1958).

Christie, N. *Crime Control as Industry* (London: Routledge, 1994).

Clarke, J. 'The Skinheads and the Magical Recovery of Community', in S. Hall and T. Jefferson (eds), *Resistance through Rituals* (London: Hutchinson, 1976), pp. 99–102.

Clarke, J. 'Football and Working-class fans: Tradition and change', in R. Ingham (ed.), *Football Hooliganism* (London: Inter-action Imprint, 1978), pp. 37–60.

Clarke, J., Hall, S., Jefferson, T. and Roberts, B. 'Subcultures, Cultures and Class', in S. Hall and T. Jefferson (eds) *Resistance through Rituals* (London: Hutchinson, 1976), pp. 9–74.

Clarke, J. and Jefferson, T. 'Working Class Youth Cultures', in G. Mungham and G. Pearson (eds), *Working Class Youth Culture* (London: Routledge & Kegan Paul, 1976), pp. 138–58.

Clarke, R. 'Situational Crime Prevention', in M. Tonry and D. Farrington (eds), *Building a Safer Society* (Chicago: University of Chicago Press, 1995), pp. 91–150.

Cloward, R. and Ohlin, L. *Delinquency and Opportunity* (Glencoe, IL: Free Press, 1960).

Cohen, A. *Delinquent Boys* (Glencoe, IL: Free Press, 1955).

Cohen, S. *Folk Devils and Moral Panics* (London: Routledge, 1972/2002).

Cohen, S. 'Campaigning against Vandalism', in C. Ward (ed.), *Vandalism* (London: The Architectural Press, 1973), pp. 215–57.

Colome, G. 'La péninsule ibérique dans la tourmente des ultras: le cas de la Catalogne', in M. Comeron (ed.), *Quels supporters pour l'an 2000?* (Brussels: Labor, 1997), pp. 82–90.

Čolović, I. *Apo tis kerkides sta charakomata* (Ioannina: Isnafi, 2007).

Comeron, M. 'Sécurité et violence dans les stades de football', *Revue de droit pénal et de criminologie* no. 9–10 (1992) 829–50.

Comeron, M. 'Du gang au groupe social: une analyse socio-préventive', *Les Cahiers de la sécurité intérieure* no. 26 (1996) 47–67.

Comeron, M. *La prévention de la violence dans le sport* (Strasbourg: Council of Europe, 2002).

Comeron, M. and Vanbellingen, P. (eds) *La prévention de la violence dans les stades de football en Europe* (Brussels: European Commission, 2002).

Cook, B. 'Football Crazy?', *New Society* (15 June 1978) 602.

Cortesi, F. *Misure antiviolenza negli stadi* (Milan: IPSOA, 2007).

Council of Europe, Recommendation 963 on Cultural and Educational Means of Reducing Violence (28 January 1983).

Council of Europe, Recommendation No. R (84)8 on the Reduction of Spectator Violence at Sporting Events and in Particular at Football Matches (19 March 1984).

Council of Europe, European Convention on Spectator Violence and Misbehaviour at Sports Events and in Particular at Football Matches, CETS no. 120 (19 August 1985).

Council of Europe, Recommendation 89/2 on Comprehensive Report on Measures to Counter Hooliganism (1989).

Council of Europe, Report on Football Hooliganism, doc. 8553 (30 September 1999a).

Council of Europe, Recommendation 1434 on Football Hooliganism (4 November 1999b).

Council of Europe, Resolution No. 4 on Preventing Racism, Xenophobia and Intolerance in Sport (30 May 2000).

Council of Europe, Recommendation Rec(2001)6 on the Prevention of Racism, Xenophobia and Racial Intolerance in Sport (18 July 2001).

Council of Europe, Recommendation 2003/1 of the Standing Committee of the European Convention on the Role of Social and Educational Measures in the Prevention of Violence in Sport and Handbook on the Prevention of Violence in Sport (2003a).

Council of Europe, Report Lesbians and Gays in Sport, doc. 9988 (22 October 2003b).

Council of the EU, Recommendation of 22 April 1996 on Guidelines for Preventing and Restraining Disorder Connected with Football Matches, *OJEC* C 131 (3 May 1996).

Council of the EU, Joint Action of 26 May 1997 with Regard to Cooperation on Law and Order and Security, *OJEC* L 147 (5 June 1997a).

Council of the EU, Resolution of 9 June 1997 on Preventing and Restraining Football Hooliganism through the Exchange of Experience, Exclusion from Stadiums and Media Policy, *OJEC* C 193 (24 June 1997b).

Council of the EU, Note from the Presidency of the Council to the Cooperation Group (experts on public order), 7386/98 ENFOPOL 45 (3 April 1998).

Council of the EU, Resolution of 21 June 1999 Concerning a Handbook for International Police Cooperation and Measures to Prevent and Control Violence and Disturbances in Connection with International Football Matches, *OJEC* C 196 (13 July 1999).

Council of the EU, Decision 2001/427/JHA of 28 May 2001 on Setting up a European Crime Prevention Network, *OJEC* L 153 (8 June 2001a).

Council of the EU, Draft Discussion Document for a Policy Debate on a Ban on Hooligans Entering and/or Leaving a Country and Similar Measures, SN 3159/01 (8 June 2001b).

Council of the EU, Conclusions Adopted by the Council and the Representatives of the Governments of the Member States on 13 July 2001 on Security at Meetings of the European Council and Other Comparable Events, Justice and Home Affairs, 10916/01 (16 July 2001c).

Council of the EU, Resolution of 6 December 2001 Concerning a Handbook with Recommendations for International Police Cooperation and Measures to Prevent and Control Violence and Disturbances in Connection with Football Matches with an International Dimension, in which at Least One Member State is Involved, *OJEC* C 22 (24 January 2002a).

Council of the EU, Decision 2002/348/JHA of 25 April 2002 Concerning Security in Connection with Football Matches with an International Dimension, *OJEC* L 121 (8 May 2002b).

Council of the EU, Resolution of 17 November 2003 on the Use by Member States of Bans on Access to Venues of Football Matches with an International Dimension, *OJEC* C 281 (22 November 2003).

Council of the EU, Resolution of 29 April 2004 on Security at European Meetings and Other Comparable Events, *OJEC* C 116 (30 April 2004).

Council of the EU, Decision 2006/.../JHA amending Decision 2002/348/JHA Concerning Security in Connection with Football Matches with an International Dimension, *OJEC* C 164/30 (15 July 2006a).

Council of the EU, Note from the Presidency of the Council to Police Cooperation Working Party, 15226/1/06, ENFOPOL 190 (22 December 2006b).

Council of the EU, Resolution of 4 December 2006 Concerning an Updated Handbook with Recommendations for International Police Cooperation and Measures to Prevent and Control Violence and Disturbances in Connection with Football Matches with an International Dimension, in which at Least One Member State is Involved, *OJEC* C 322 (29 December 2006c).

Council of the EU, Decision 2007/412/JHA of 12 June 2007 amending Decision 2002/348/JHA Concerning Security in Connection with Football Matches with an International Dimension, *OJEC* L 155 (15 June 2007a).

Council of the EU, Draft Council Conclusions Adopting the Work Programme on Further Measures Designed to Maximise Safety and Security in Connection with Football Matches with an International Dimension, 15615/07 ENFOPOL 198 (23 November 2007b).

Courakis, N. Report on the Incidence of Violence at Greek Sports Stadiums, XIII Informal Meeting of European Ministers of Sport, Council of Europe (Athens, 1988).

Courakis, N. 'Football Violence: Not only a British problem', *European Journal on Criminal Policy and Research* 6 (1998) 293–302.

Crabbe, T. 'The Public Gets what the Public Wants. England football fans, "truth" claims and mediated realities', *International Review for the Sociology of Sport* 38(4) (2003) 413–25.

Crewe, I. 'Values: the crusade that failed', in D. Kavanagh and A. Seldon (eds), *The Thatcher Effect* (Oxford: Oxford University Press, 1989), pp. 239–50.

Critcher, C. *Moral Panics and the Media* (Buckingham: Open University Press, 2003).

Crouch, C. and Pizzorno, A. (eds) *The Resurgence of Class Conflict in Western Europe since 1968* (London: Macmillan, 1978).

Cusson, M. 'Examen critique des théories sous culturelles de la délinquance juvénile', *Annales de Vaucresson* no. 18 (1981) 275–91.

Dal Lago, A. *Descrizione di una battaglia* (Bologna: Il Mulino, 1990a).

Dal Lago, A. 'Ermeneutica del calcio', *Rassegna italiana di sociologia* 3 (1990b) 293–323.

Dal Lago, A. *Non-persone* (Milan: Feltrinelli, 1999).

Dal Lago, A. and De Biasi, R. 'Italian Football Fans. Culture and organization', in R. Giulianotti, N. Bonney and M. Hepworth (eds), *Football, Violence and Social Identity* (London: Routledge, 1994), pp. 73–89.

Dal Lago, A. and Moscati, R. *Regalateci un sogno* (Milan: Bompiani, 1992).

De Biasi, R. 'Ordre public et tifosi', *Les Cahiers de la sécurité intérieure* no. 26 (1996) 75–91.

De Biasi, R. 'The Policing of Hooliganism in Italy', in D. Della Porta and H. Reiter (eds), *Policing Protest* (Minneapolis: University of Minnesota Press, 1998), pp. 213–27.

De Biasi, R. 'Il tifo calcistico', in A. Dal Lago and R. De Biasi (eds), *Un certo sguardo* (Rome: Laterza, 2002), pp. 104–30.

Debuyst, C. 'Etiologie de la violence', in *La violence dans la société* (Strasbourg: Council of Europe, 1974), pp. 187–267.

De Giorgi, A. *Zero tolleranza* (Rome: Derive Approdi, 2000).

De Leo, G. 'La violenza fra rumore e mesaggio. Un itinerario di ricerca sulla rappresentazione del tifo nella stampa', in A. Salvini (ed.), *Il rito aggressivo* (Florence: Giunti, 1988), pp. 274–99.

Della Porta, D. *Social Movements, Political Violence and the State* (New York: Cambridge University Press, 1995).

Della Porta, D. 'Police Knowledge and Protest Policing: Some reflections on the Italian case', in D. Della Porta and H. Reiter (eds), *Policing Protest* (Minneapolis: University of Minnesota Press, 1998), pp. 228–52.

Della Porta, D. and Reiter, H. 'Da polizia del "governo" a polizia "dei cittadini"? Le politiche dell'ordine pubblico in Italia', *Stato e Mercato* 48(3) (1996) 433–65.

Della Porta, D. and Reiter, H. (eds) *Policing Protest* (Minneapolis: University of Minnesota Press, 1998).

Delmas-Marty, M. *Modèles et mouvements de politique criminelle* (Paris: Economica, 1983).

Delmas-Marty, M. 'Le paradoxe pénal', in M. Delmas-Marty and C. Lucas de Leyssac (eds). *Libertés et droits fondamentaux* (Paris: Seuil, 2002), pp. 437–61.

De Valkeneer, C. 'Les nouvelles stratégies policières: aux confins des criminalisations primaire et secondaire', in F. Tulkens (ed.), *Acteur social et délinquance* (Liège: Mardaga, 1990), pp. 310–25.

Dillon, M. 'Virtual Security: a life science of (dis)order', *Millenium* 32(3) (2003) 531–58.

Docters van Leeuwen, A. 'Comments on "Riots without Killings"', *Contemporary Crises* 14(4) (1990) 377–80.

Dorn, N. and Levi, M. 'European Private Security, Corporate Investigation and Military Services: Collective security, market regulation and structuring the public sphere', *Policing & Society* 17(3) (2007) 213–38.

Downes, G. 'The Case for Going Dutch: the lessons of postwar penal policy', *The Political Quarterly* 63(1) (1992) 12–24.

Dubet, F. *La galère* (Paris: Fayard, 1987).

Dunand, M. 'Violence et panique dans le stade de football de Bruxelles en 1985: approche psycho-sociale des événements', *Revue de droit pénal et de criminologie* no. 5 (1987) 403–40.

Dunning, E. (ed.) *The Sociology of Sport* (London: Frank Cass, 1971).

Dunning, E. 'The Social Roots of Football Hooliganism: a reply to the critics of the "Leicester School"', in R. Giulianotti, N. Bonney and M. Hepworth (eds), *Football, Violence and Social Identity* (London: Routledge, 1994), pp. 128–57. .

Dunning, E. *Sport Matters* (London: Routledge, 1999).

Dunning, E. 'Towards a Sociological Understanding of Football Hooliganism as a World Phenomenon', *European Journal on Criminal Policy and Research* 8 (2000) 141–62.

Dunning, E., Murphy, P. and Newburn, T. 'Violent Disorders in Twentieth-century Britain', in G. Gaskell and R. Benewick (eds), *The Crowd in Contemporary Britain* (London: Sage, 1987), pp. 19–75.

Dunning, E., Murphy, P. and Waddington, I. 'Anthropological versus Sociological Approaches to the Study of Soccer Hooliganism: Some critical notes', *The Sociological Review* 39(3) (1991) 459–78.

Dunning, E., Murphy, P. and Waddington, I. 'Towards a Sociological Understanding of Foiotball Hooliganism as a World Phenomenon', in E. Dunning et al. (eds), *Fighting Fans* (Dublin: University College Dublin Press, 2002), pp. 1–22.

Dunning, E., Murphy, P. and Williams, J. 'Spectator Violence at Football Matches: Towards a sociological explanation', in N. Elias and E. Dunning (eds), *Quest for Excitement* (Oxford: Blackwell, 1986a), pp. 245–66.

Dunning, E., Murphy, P. and Williams, J. ' "Casuals", "Terrace Crews" and "Fighting Firms": Towards a sociological explanation of football hooligan behaviour', in D. Riches (ed.), *The Anthropology of Violence* (Oxford: Blackwell, 1986b), pp. 164–83.

Dunning, E., Murphy, P. and Williams, J. *The Roots of Football Hooliganism* (London: Routledge & Kegan Paul, 1988).

Edelman, M. *Constructing the Political Spectacle* (Chicago: University of Chicago Press, 1988).

Ehrenberg, A. 'Le football et ses imaginaires', *Les Temps Modernes* no. 460 (1984) 841–5.

Ehrenberg, A. 'Les hooligans ou la passion d'être égal', *Esprit* no. 104/105 (1985) 7–13.

Ehrenberg, A. 'La rage de paraître', *Autrement* no. 80 (1986) 148–58.

Ehrenberg, A. *Le culte de la performance* (Paris: Calmann-Lévy, 1991).

Ehrenberg, A., Chartier, R. and Augé, M. 'Sport, religion et violence', *Esprit* no. 4 (1987) 63–70.

Elias, N. and Dunning, E. (eds) *Quest for Excitement* (Oxford: Blackwell, 1986).

Erbes, J., Monet, J., Funk, A. et al. *Polices d'Europe* (Paris: IHESI/L'Harmattan, 1992).

Ericson, R. V. *Crime in an Insecure World* (Cambridge: Polity, 2007).

Ericson, R. V. and Haggerty, K. *Policing the Risk Society* (Oxford: Oxford University Press, 1997).

Erikson, K. T. *Wayward Puritans* (New York: John Wiley, 1966).

Erkiner, K. 'Les problèmes posés par les spectateurs turcs à l'intérieur et à l'extérieur des stades. Dimensions nationale et internationale', in D. Yarsuvat and P.–H. Bolle (eds), *La violence et le fanatisme dans le sport* (Istanbul: University of Galatasaray, 2004), pp. 181–207.

Escriva, J.–P. and Vaugrand, H. (eds) *L'opium sportif* (Paris: L'Harmattan, 1996).

Esman, C. and Adang, O. *Inventarisation of social preventive projects in the Netherlands* (Apeldoorn: Police Academy of the Netherlands, 2005).

Esterle-Hedibel, M. 'Jeunes des cités, police et désordres urbains', in L. Mucchielli and P. Robert (eds), *Crime et sécurité, l'état des savoirs* (Paris: La Découverte, 2002), pp. 376–85.

European Commission, Communication, The Prevention of Crime in the European Union: Reflection on common guidelines and proposals for Community financial support, Proposal for a Council Decision establishing a programme of incentives and exchanges, training and cooperation for the prevention of crime, COM(2000) 786 final, 2000/0304 (CNS) (29 November 2000).

European Commission, Proposed Council Decision on the Creation of the European Police Office (Europol), COM/2006/0817 final – CNS 2006/0310 (20 December 2006).

European Commission, *White Paper on Sport*, COM(2007) 391 final (11 July 2007).

European Parliament, Resolution on Sport in the Community, *OJEC* C 127 (14 May 1984).

European Parliament, Resolution of 11 July 1985 on the Measures Meeded to Combat Vandalism and Violence in Sport, *OJEC* C 229 (9 September1985a).

European Parliament, Resolution of 13 November 1985 on Europe of the Citizens, *OJEC* C 345 (31 December 1985b).

European Parliament, Resolution of 22 January 1988 on Vandalism and Violence in Sport, *OJEC* C 49 (22 February 1988).

European Parliament, Report of the Committee of Inquiry into Racism and Xenophobia, *OJEC* C 284 (12 November 1990).

European Parliament, Resolution on the EU and Sport, *OJEC* C 205 (25 July 1994).

European Parliament, Committee on Civil Liberties and Home Affairs, Report on Football Hooliganism and on the Freedom of Movement of Football Supporters, Doc. A4–0124/96 (25 April 1996a).

European Parliament, Debate on Hooliganism and the Free Movement of Football Supporters (sitting of 21 May 1996b).

European Parliament, Resolution of 21 May 1996 on Hooliganism and the Free Movement of Football Supporters, *OJEC* C 166 (10 June 1996c).

European Parliament, Resolution on Euro 2000, *OJEC* C 121 (24 April 2000).

European Parliament, Recommendation to the Council on a Space of Freedom, Security and Justice: Security at meetings of the European Council and other comparable events (2001/2167(INI)), doc. A5–0396/2001 (12 December 2001).

European Parliament, Debate on the Draft Council Decision Concerning Security in Connection with Football Matches with an International Dimension (sitting of 8 April 2002).

European Parliament, Report on the Initiative by the Republic of Austria with a View to the Adoption of a Council Decision Amending Decision 2002/348/JHA Concerning Security in Connection with Football Matches with an International Dimension, doc. A6–0052/2007 (2007a).

European Parliament, Debate on the Future of Professional Football in Europe – Security at football matches (sitting of 28 March 2007b).

European Parliament, legislative resolution of 29 March 2007 on the Initiative by the Republic of Austria with a View to the Adoption of a Council Decision Amending Decision 2002/348/JHA Concerning Security in Connection with Football Matches with an International Dimension (10543/2006 – C6–0240/2006 – 2006/0806(CNS) (2007c).

Ewald, F. *L'Etat-providence* (Paris: Grasset, 1986).

Federazione Italiana Giuoco Calcio (FIGC) *Rapports entre les clubs de football et les clubs des supporters* (Rome: FIGC, 1988).

Feeley, M. 'Crime, Social Order and the Rise of neo-Conservative Politics', *Theoretical Criminology* 7(1) (2003) 111–30.

Feeley, M. and Simon, J. 'The New Penology: Notes on the emerging strategy of corrections and its implications', *Criminology* 30(4) (1992) 449–74.

Fijnaut, C. and Marx, G. T. (eds) *Undercover-Police Surveillance in Comparative Perspective* (Norwell: Kluwer Academic Publishers, 1995).

Fillieule, O. and Della Porta, D. (eds) *Police et manifestants* (Paris: Presses de Sciences Po, 2006).

Finn, G. 'Football Violence: A societal psychological perspective', in R. Giulianotti, N. Bonney and M. Hepworth (eds), *Football, Violence and Social Identity* (London: Routledge, 1994), pp. 90–127.

Foucault, M. *Histoire de la folie à l'âge classique* (Paris: Gallimard, 1961).

Foucault, M. *Surveiller et punir* (Paris: Gallimard, 1975).

Foucault, M. 'Deux essais sur le sujet et le pouvoir', in H. Dreyfus and P. Rabinow (eds), *Michel Foucault. Un parcours philosophique* (Paris: Gallimard, 1984), pp. 297–321.

Foucault, M. *Il faut défendre la société* (Paris: Gallimard/Seuil, 1997).

Frattini, F. 'Closing Intervention on Violence in Sport', High level conference *Towards an EU Strategy against Violence in Sport*, Brussels (29 November 2007).

Free, M. and Hughson, J. 'Settling Accounts with Hooligans. Gender blindness in football supporter subculture research', *Men and Masculinities* 6(2) (2003) 136–55.

Froment, J.-C. and Kaluszynski, M. (eds) *Justice et technologies* (Grenoble: PUG, 2006).

Frosdick, S. and Marsh, P. *Football Hooliganism* (Cullompton: Willan Publishing, 2005).

Garland, D. *Punishment and Welfare* (Aldershot: Gower, 1985).

Garland, D. 'The Limits of the Sovereign State. Strategies of Crime Control in Contemporary Society', *The British Journal of Criminology* 36(4) (1996) 445–71.

Garland, J. and Rowe, M. 'War Minus the Shooting? Jingoism, the English press, and Euro 96', *Journal of Sport & Social Issues* 23(1) (1999a) 80–95.

Garland, J. and Rowe, M. 'Policing Racism at Football Matches: An assessment of recent developments in police strategies', *International Journal of the Sociology of the Law* 27(3) (1999b) 251–66.

Garland, J. and Rowe, M. 'The Hooligans' Fear of the Penalty', *Soccer and Society* 1(1) (2000) 144–57.

Gaxie, D. 'Economie des partis et rétributions du militantisme', *Revue française de science politique* 27(1) (1997) 123–54.

Gill, P. *Rounding up the Usual Suspects?* (Burlington, VA: Ashgate, 2000).

Girard, R. *La violence et le sacré* (Paris: Grasset, 1972).

Giulianotti, R. 'Scotland's Tartan Army in Italy: the case for the carnivalesque', *The Sociological Review* 39(3) (1991) 503–27.

Giulianotti, R. 'Social Identity and Public Order: Political and academic discourses on football violence', in R. Giulianotti, N. Bonney and M. Hepworth (eds), *Football, Violence and Social Identity* (London: Routledge, 1994), pp. 10–36.

Giulianotti, R. 'Football and the Politics of Carnival: an ethnographic study of Scottish fans in Sweden', *International Review for the Sociology of Sport* 30(2) (1995) 191–223.

Giulianotti, R. and Gerrard, M. 'Cruel Britannia? Glasgow, Rangers, Scotland and "hot" football rivalries', in G. Armstrong and R. Giulianotti (eds), *Fear and Loathing in World Football* (Oxford: Berg, 2001), pp. 23–42.

Goffman, E. *Asiles* (Paris: Minuit, 1968).

Goffman, E. *La mise en scène de la vie quotidienne* (Paris: Minuit, 1973).

Golfinopoulos, Y. *Ellinas pote* (Ioannina: Isnafi, 2007).

Goode, E. and Ben-Yehuda, N. *Moral Panics* (Oxford: Blackwell, 1994).

Govaert, S. and Comeron, M. *Foot & Violence* (Brussels: De Boeck Université, 1995).

Graham, S. and Wood, D. 'Digitizing Surveillance: Categorization, space, inequality', *Critical Social Policy* 23(2) (2003) 227–48.

Graziano, L. and Tarrow, S. (eds) *La crisi italiana* (Torino: Einaudi, 1979).

Greenfield, S. and Osborn, G. 'England's Dreaming: the legal regulation of the space(s) and place(s) of football and cricket', Conference *Collective Identities and Symbolic Representations*, Paris, 3–6 July 1996.

Greenfield, S. and Osborn, G. 'When the Writ Hits the Fan: Panic law and football fandom', in A. Brown (ed.), *Fanatics! Power, Identity & Fandom in Football* (London: Routledge, 1998), pp. 235–48.

Greenfield, S. and Osborn, G. *Regulating Football* (London: Pluto Press, 2001).

Groenevelt, H. 'La gestion de l'information: support préventif à la sécurité', in M. Comeron and P. Vanbellingen (eds), *La prévention de la violence dans les stades de football en Europe* (Brussels: European Commission, 2002), pp. 135–40.

Guild, E. 'Agamben face aux juges. Souveraineté, exception et antiterrorisme', *Cultures & Conflits* no. 51 (2003a) 127–56.

Guild, E. 'Exceptionalism and Transnationalism: UK judicial control of the detention of foreign "international terrorists"', *Alternatives* 28 (2003b) 491–515.

Hahn, E. 'Violence of Football Spectators – Relevance, Scientific Research, and Treatment in the Federal Republic of Germany', European Congress *Violence Control in the World of Sports*, Athens, 17–19 February 1989.

Hall, S. 'The Treatment of Football Hooliganism in the Press', in R. Ingham (ed.), *Football Hooliganism* (London: Inter-action Imprint, 1978), pp. 15–36.

Hall, S., Critcher, C., Jefferson, T. et al. *Policing the Crisis* (Basingstoke: Palgrave Macmillan, 1978).

Haubrich, D. 'September 11, Anti-Terror Laws and Civil Liberties: Britain, France and Germany compared', *Government and Opposition* 38(1) (2003) 3–28.

Hermes, J. 'Burnt Orange: Television, football, and the representation of ethnicity', *Television New Media* 6(1) (2005) 49–69.

Hirschi, T. *Causes of Delinquency* (Berkeley, CA: University of California Press, 1969).

Hirschman, A. *Exit, Voice and Loyalty* (Harvard, MA: Harvard University Press, 1970).

Hobbs, D. Robins, D. 'The Boy Done Good: Football violence, changes and continuities', *The Sociological Review* 39(3) (1991) 551–79.

Hodges, A. and Nilep, C. (eds) *Discourse, War and Terrorism* (Amsterdam: John Benjamins, 2007).

Hoggart, R. *The Uses of Literacy* (Harmondsworth: Penguin Books, 1986, first published 1957).

Hörnqvist, M. 'The Birth of Public Order Policy', *Race & Class* 46(1) (2004) 30–52.

Houchon, G. 'Propos optimistes d'un abolitionnisme morose', in F. Tulkens and H. D. Bosly (eds), *La justice pénale et l'Europe* (Brussels: Bruylant, 1996), pp. 75–101.

Hourcade, N. 'L'engagement politique des supporters "ultras" français. Retour sur les idées reçues', *Politix* no. 50 (2000) 107–25.

Hughes, M. 'German Authorities Call on Awacs to Counter Hooligans', *The Times* (12 October 2005) <www.timesonline.co.uk>.

Huysmans, J. 'Migrants as a Security Problem: Dangers of "securitizing" societal issues', in R. Mils and D. Thrännhardt (eds), *Migration and European Integration* (London: Pinter, 1995), pp. 53–72.

Huysmans, J. 'A Foucaultian View on Spill-over: Freedom and security in the EU', *Journal of International Relations and Development* 7(3) (2004) 294–318.

Huysmans, J. *The Politics of Insecurity* (London: Routledge, 2006).

Ingham, R. 'A Social Psychological Analysis of British Football Hooliganism', European Congress, *Violence Control in the World of Sports*, Athens, 17–19 February 1989.

Ingram, R. 'The Psychology of the Crowd – A Social Psychological Analysis of British Football Hooliganism', *Medicine, Science and the Law* 25(1) (1985) 53–8.

Inthorn, S. 'The Death of the Hun? National identity and German press coverage of the 1998 football World Cup', *European Journal of Cultural Studies* 5(1) (2002) 49–68.

Jenkins, P. *Intimate Enemies* (New York: Aldine de Gruyter, 1992).

Jewkes, Y. *Media & Crime* (London: Sage, 2004).

Johnson, R. 'Defending Ways of Life', *Theory, Culture & Society* 19(4) (2002) 211–31.

Johnston, L. and Shearing, C. *Governing Security* (London: Routledge, 2003).

Jones, R. 'Digital rule. Punishment, control and technology', *Punishment & Society* 2(1) (2000) 5–22.

Jones, T. *Policing and Democracy in the Netherlands* (London: Policy Studies Institute, 1995).

Kearney, R. 'Terror, Philosophy and the Sublime. Some philosophical reflections on 11 September', *Philosophy & Social Criticism* 29(1) (2003) 23–51.

Kellens, G. 'La socio-prévention offensive en matière de délinquance juvénile', in M. Comeron (ed.), *Quels supporters pour l'an 2000?* (Brussels: Labor, 1997) pp. 199–24.

Kerr, J. *Understanding Soccer Hooliganism* (Buckingham: Open University Press, 1994).

King, A. 'Outline of a Practical Theory of Football Violence', *Sociology* 29(4) (1995) 635–51.

Kokoreff, M. *La force des quartiers* (Paris: Payot, 2003).

Koren, R. *Les enjeux éthiques de l'écriture de presse et la mise en mots du terrorisme* (Paris: L'Harmattan, 1996).

Koukouris, K. and Taxildaridis, S. 'Aggression against Referees in Greek Basketball. Referees' perspective on violent incidents in Greek basketball', in D. Panagiotopoulos (ed.), *Sports Law* (Athens: Sakkoulas, 2005), pp. 258–65.

Koukouris, K., Taxildaridis, S., Zarabouka, O. et al. 'Differences in the phenomenon of sport violences in Greek and European basketball championships', Pre-Olympic Congress, ICSSPE, Thessaloniki, 6–11 August 2004.

Lacombe, D. 'Les liaisons dangereuses. Foucault et la criminologie', *Criminologie* 26(1) (1993) 51–72.

Lagrange, H. *Demandes de sécurité* (Paris: Seuil, 2003).

Lamberti, A. *Il diritto contro la violenza nel mondo del calcio* (Rome: Società Stampa Sportiva, 1988).

Lawrence, R. *The Politics of Force* (Berkeley, CA: University of California Press, 2000).

Lazar, A. and Lazar, M. 'The Discourse of the New World Order: "Out-casting" the double face of threat', *Discourse & Society* 15(2–3) (2004) 223–42.

Leben, C. 'De quelques doctrines de l'ordre juridique', *Droits* no. 33 (2001) 19–39.

Lemert, E. 'Social Structure, Social Control and Deviation', in M. B. Clinard (ed.), *Anomie and Deviant Behavior* (New York: The Free Press, 1964), pp. 57–97.

Lemert, E. *Human Deviance, Social Problems and Social Control* (Englewood Cliffs, NJ: Prentice Hall, 1967).

Le Noé, O. 'Football et violences', *Regards sur l'actualité* no. 243 (1998) 55–70.

Leone, R. and Anrig, G. (eds) *The War on our Freedoms* (New York: Public Affairs, 2003).

Leudar, I., Marsland, V. and Nekvapil, J. 'On Membership Categorization: "Us", "them" and "doing violence" in political discourse', *Discourse & Society* 15(2–3) (2004) 243–66.

Lévy, R. and Zauberman, R. 'De quoi la République a-t-elle peur? Police, Blacks et Beurs', *Mouvements* no. 4 (1999) 39–46.

Lewis, J. 'Crowd Control at English Football Matches', *Sociological Focus* 15(4) (1980) 417–23.

Leyens, J. and Rimé, B. 'Violence dans les stades: la réponse des psychologies', *La Recherche* 19 (1988) 528–31.

Liberty, Briefing on the Draft Football (Disorder) Bill (July 2000) <www.liberty-human-rights.org.uk>.

Limbergen, K. van, Colaers, C. and Walgrave, L. *The Societal and Psycho-Sociological Background of Football Hooliganism* (Louvain: University of Louvain, 1987).

Limbergen, K. van and Walgrave, L. 'Aspects sociopsychologiques de l'hooliganisme: une vision criminologique', *Pouvoirs* no. 61 (1992) 117–30.

Lipshutz, R. (ed.) *On Security* (New York: Columbia University Press, 1995).

Loader, I. 'Plural Policing and Democratic Governance', *Social & Legal Studies* 9(3) (2000) 323–45.

Loader, I. and Walker, N. 'Necessary Virtues: the legitimate place of the state in the production of security', in B. Dupont and J. Wood (eds), *Democracy, Society and the Governance of Security* (Cambridge: Cambridge University Press, 2006), pp. 165–95.

Loader, I. and Walker, N. *Civilizing Security* (Cambridge: Cambridge University Press, 2007).

Louis S. *Le phénomène ultras en Italie* (Paris: Mare & Martin, 2006).

Louis S. 'Le mouvement ultras en Italie au tournant des XXe et XXIe siècles', unpublished PhD thesis, University of Perpignan, 2008.

Luhmann, N. *I pragmatikotita ton meson mazikis epikoinonias* [original title: *Die Realität der Massenmedien*] (Athens: Metaichmio, 2003).

Lyon, D. *The Electronic Eye* (Cambridge: Polity, 1994).

Lyon, D. *Surveillance Society* (Buckingham: Open University Press, 2001).

Lyon, D. 'Globalizing Surveillance. Comparative and sociological perspectives', *International Sociology* 19(2) (2004) 135–49.

Maguire, J. and Poulton, E. 'The War of the Words? Identity politics in Anglo-German press coverage of Euro 96', *European Journal of Communication* 14(1) (1999a) 61–89.

Maguire, J. and Poulton, E. 'European Identity Politics in Euro 96: Invented traditions and national habitus codes', *International Review for the Sociology of Sport* 34(1) (1999b) 17–29.

Maguire, J., Poulton, E. and Possamai, C. 'Weltkrieg III? Media coverage of England versus Germany in Euro 96', *Journal of Sport & Social Issues* 23(4) (1999) 439–54.

Maigret, E. *Sociologie de la communication et des medias* (Paris: Armand Colin, 2004).

Marchi, V. *Il derby del bambino morto* (Rome: DeriveApprodi, 2005).

Marenin, O. (ed.) *Policing Change, Changing Police* (New York: Garland Press, 1995).

Margaritis, G. and Metaxas, I. (eds) *Historia ton Hellinon* (vol. 17–18) (Athens: Domi, 2006).

Marivoet, S. 'Violent Disturbances in Portuguese Football', in E. Dunning P. Murphy, I. Waddington et al. (eds), *Fighting Fans* (Dublin: University College Dublin Press, 2002), pp. 158–73.

Mark, J. and Pearson, G. 'Football Banning Orders: Analysing their use in court', *Journal of Criminal Law* 70(6) (2006) 509–30.

Marsh, P. 'Understanding Aggro', *New Society* (3 April 1975) 7–9.

Marsh, P. 'Careers for Boys: Nutters, hooligans and hardcases', *New Society* (13 May 1976) 346–8.

Marsh, P. 'Novices, Rowdies and Graduates: the social order of the terraces', *The Listener* (19 May 1977a) 644–6.

Marsh, P. 'Football Hooliganism: Fact or fiction?', *British Journal of Law and Society* 4(2) (1977b) 256–9.

Marsh, P. *Aggro: The Illusion of Violence* (London: Dent, 1978).

Marsh, P. and Campbell, A. (eds) *Aggression and Violence* (Oxford: Blackwell, 1982).

Marsh, P., Rosser, E. and Harré, R. *The Rules of Disorder* (London: Routledge & Kegan Paul, 1978).

Marshall, I. H. (ed.) *Minorities, Migrants and Crime* (London: Sage, 1997).

Marshall, P. 'A New British Export – Football Hooliganism', *The Listener* (5 July 1984) 5.

Martinson, R. 'What Works? Questions and answers about prison reform', *The Public Interest* no. 35 (1974) 22–54.

Mary, P. 'La pénalisation du social', in P. Mary and T. Papatheodorou (eds), *Crime et insécurité en Europe* (Brussels: Bruylant, 2001) pp. 7–23.

Mary, P. *Insécurité et pénalisation du social* (Brussels: Labor, 2003).

Mary, P. and Papatheodorou, T. (eds) *Crime et insécurité en Europe* (Brussels: Bruylant, 2001).

Massé, M. 'L'espace Schengen. Développement de l'entraide répressive internationale', *Revue de science criminelle et de droit pénal comparé* no. 4 (1992) 800–8.

Mastrogiannakis, D. 'Luttes et enjeux pour la définition de la sécurité dans les stades grecs', in C. Jaccoud et al. (eds), *Violence et extrémisme dans le football* (Lausanne: Antipodes, 2008), pp. 241–52.

Matza, D. *Delinquency and Drift* (New York: Wiley, 1964).

Melossi, D. and Pavarini, M. *The Prison and the Factory* (Basingstoke: Macmillan, 1981).

Merton, R. *Social Theory and Social Structure* (Glencoe, IL: The Free Press, 1957).

Merton, R. 'Anomie, Anomia and Social Interaction: Contexts of deviant behavior', in M. B. Clinard (ed.), *Anomie and Deviant Behavior* (New York: The Free Press, 1964), pp. 213–42.

Miège C., 'La lutte contre la violence dans le sport au sein de l'Union Européenne', *Regards sur l'actualité* no. 285 (2002) 79–92.

Mignon, P. *La société du samedi : supporters, ultras et hooligans*, Final Report (Paris: Interior Ministry, 1993).

Mignon, P. 'La lutte contre le hooliganisme. Comparaisons européennes', *Les Cahiers de la sécurité intérieure* no. 26 (1996) 92–107.

Mignon, P. *La passion du football* (Paris: Odile Jacob, 1998).

Mignon, P. and Tsoukala, A. *Etude comparée des dispositifs de lutte contre le hooliganisme: Grande-Bretagne, Allemagne, Pays-Bas, Belgique*, Final Report (Paris: Interior Ministry, 1996).

Mojet, H. 'The European Union and Football Hooliganism', *The International Sports Law Journal* no. 1–2 (2005) 69–77.

Monjardet, D. *Ce que fait la police* (Paris: La Découverte, 1996).

Moorhouse, H. F. 'Professional Football and Working Class Culture: English theories and Scottish evidence', *The Sociological Review* 32(2) (1984) 285–315.

Moorhouse, H. F. 'From Zines Like These? Fanzines, tradition and identity in Scottish football', in G. Jarvie and G. Walker (eds), *Scottish Sport in the Making of the Nation* (Leicester: Leicester University Press, 1994), pp. 173–94.

Moorhouse, H. F. 'Book Review on "Football Hooligans. Knowing the score" (Armstrong 1998)', *Urban Studies* 37(8) (2000) pp. 1463–4.

Morris, D. *The Soccer Tribe* (London: Jonathan Cape, 1981).

Mucchielli, L. *Violences et insécurité* (Paris: La Découverte, 2001).

Mucchielli, L., Lévy, R. and Zauberman, R. (eds) *Crime et insécurité* (Paris: L'Harmattan, 2006).

Muncie, J. *The Trouble with Kids Today* (London: Hutchinson, 1984).

Murphy, P., Dunning, E. and Williams, J. 'Soccer Crowd Disorder and the Press: Processes of amplification and de-amplification in historical perspective', *Theory, Culture, Society* 5 (1988) 645–73.

Murphy, P., Williams, J. and Dunning, E. *Football on Trial* (London: Routledge, 1990).

National Consultative Committee on Football Hooliganism, *Combating Football Hooliganism*, Final Report (The Hague: Publishing Office of the Association of Netherlands Municipalities, 1987).

Néré, J. *Les crises économiques au XXᵉ siècle* (Paris: Armand Colin, 1989).

Neveu, E. *Sociologie du journalisme* (Paris: La Découverte, 2001/2004).

Nikolopoulos, G. *Kratos, poiniki exousia kai evropaiki oloklirosi* (Athens: Kritiki, 2002).

Nogala, D. 'Le marché de la sécurité privée: Analyse d'une évolution internationale', *Les Cahiers de la sécurité intérieure* no. 24 (1996) 121–37.

Norris, C., Moran, J. and Armstrong, G. (eds) *Surveillance, Closed Circuit Television and Social Control* (Aldershot: Ashgate, 1998).

Nuytens, W. 'La violence des supporters autonomes: à la recherche de causalités', in J.–C. Basson (ed.), *Sport et ordre public* (Paris: IHESI/La Documentation française, 2001), pp. 127–44.

Nuytens, W. 'La violence dans les stades de football. Eléments d'étiologie à partir du cas des autonomes du Racing Club de Lens', *Revue internationale de criminologie et de police technique et scientifique* LV (2002) 277–300.

Nuytens, W. *La popularité du football* (Arras: Artois Presses Université, 2004).

Nuytens, W. 'Le supporter de football et la règle: entre la faire et la défaire', *Déviance et Société* 29(2) (2005) 155–66.

Nuytens, W. 'Footballeurs, supporters et violences', *Esporte e Sociedade* no. 7 (11/2007–02/2008) <http://www.esporteesociedade.com>.

Obershall, A. *Social Conflict and Social Movements* (Englewood Cliffs, NJ: Prentice-Hall, 1973).

Olson, M. *The Logic of Collective Action* (Cambridge MA: Harvard University Press, 1965).

O'Neill, M. 'Policing Football in Scotland', *International Review for the Sociology of Sport* 39(1) (2004) 95–104.

O'Neill, M. *Policing Football* (Basingstoke: Palgrave Macmillan, 2006).

Onofri, M. and Ricci, A. 'I ragazzi della curva', *Il Mulino* 295(5) (1984) 813–35.

Osborne, D. and Gaebler, T. *Reinventing Government* (New York: Plume, 1993).

Ottenhof, R. 'Le crime organisé: de la notion criminologique à la notion juridique', in Institut de Sciences Pénales et de Criminologie, *Criminalité organisée et ordre dans la société* (Marseille: Presses Universitaires d'Aix, 1997), pp. 45–8.

Palidda, S. (ed.) *Immigrant Delinquency* (Brussels: European Commission, 1997).

Palidda, S. 'Polizia e immigrati: un'analisi etnografica', *Rassegna Italiana di Sociologia* no. 1 (1999) 77–114.

Papageorgiou, D. *Mia 'alli' Kyriaki* (Thessalonica: Paratiritis, 1998).

Papatheodorou, T. and Mary, P. (eds) *Mutations des politiques criminelles en Europe* (Athens: Papazissis, 2006).

Pearson, G. *Hooligan: A History of Respectable Fears* (London: Macmillan, 1983).

Pearson, G. 'Legitimate Targets? The civil liberties of football fans', *Journal of Civil Liberties* 4(1) (1999) 28–47.

Pearson, G. 'Qualifying for Europe? The legitimacy of football banning orders "on complaint" under the principle of proportionality', *Entertainment & Sports Law Journal* 1 (2005) <www.warwick.ac.uk>.

Peelo, M. and Soothill, K. 'The Place of Public Narratives in Reproducing Social Order', *Theoretical Criminology* 4(2) (2000), 131–48.

Peralva, A. and Macé, E. *Médias et violences urbaines* (Paris: La Documentation française/IHESI, 2002).

Peristianis, N. (ed.) *Via sta gipeda* (Nicosia: Intercollege, 2002).

Perryman, M. *Ingerland* (London: Simon & Schuster, 2006).

Pilz, G. 'Social Factors Influencing Sport and Violence: On the problem of football hooliganism in Germany', *International Review for the Sociology of Sport* 31(1) (1996) 49–68.

Poulton, E. 'Tears, Tantrums and Tattoos: Framing the hooligan', in M. Perryman (ed.), *Hooligan Wars* (Edinburgh: Mainstream Publishing, 2002) pp. 122–38.

Poulton, E. 'English Media Representation of Football-related Disorder: "Brutal, short-hand and simplifying"?', *Sport in Society* 8(1) (2005) 27–47.

Pratt, J. 'Beyond "Gulags Western Style"? A reconsideration of Nils Christie's crime control as industry', *Theoretical Criminology* 5(3) (2001) 283–314.

Progetto ultra, *Il Manualetto di sopravvivenza del tifoso* <www.progettoultra.it>.

Ramonet, I. 'Le football, c'est la guerre', *Le Monde diplomatique* (July 1990) 7.

Rasmussen, M. V. 'A Parallel Globalization of Terror: 9–11, security and globalization', *Cooperation and Conflict* 37(3) (2002) 323–49.

Raspaud, M. 'Le mondiale de la castagne et de la bêtise?', *Révolution* no. 537 (1990) 20–2.

Redeker, R. *Le sport contre les peuples* (Paris: Berg International, 2002).

Redhead, S. 'Some Reflections on Discourses on Football Hooliganism', *The Sociological Review* 39(3) (1991) 479–86.

Redhead, S. *Post-Fandom and the Millennial Blues* (London: Routledge, 1997).

Reiner, R. 'Crime and Control in Britain', *Sociology* 34(1) (2000) 71–94.

Report by the Committee on a People's Europe, *Bulletin of the European Communities* no. suppl. 7/85 (1985) 18–30.

Rey, J. and Pérez Grijelmo, D. 'Football Hooliganism – National and International/Transnational Aspects', *The International Sports Law Journal*, no. 3–4 (2004) 33–8.

Richard, J.–A. 'Mondial: la justice-carton rouge', *Le Figaro* (2 July 1998) 8C.

Rigakos, G. and Hadden, R. 'Crime, Capitalism and the "Risk Society". Towards the same olde modernity?', *Theoretical Criminology* 5(1) (2001) 61–84.

Rimé, B., Dunand, M., Boulanger, B. et al. 'Eléments pour l'analyse des événements du Heysel survenus le 29 mai 1985 à Bruxelles', *Revue interdisciplinaire d'études juridiques*, special issue (1988) 47–59.

Robert, P. and Faugeron, C. *Les forces cachées de la justice* (Paris: Centurion, 1980).

Rose, N. and Miller, P. 'Political Power beyond the State: Problematics of government', *British Journal of Sociology* 43(2) (1992) 173–205.

Rosner Kornhauser, R. *Social Sources of Delinquency* (Chicago: University of Chicago Press, 1984, first published 1978).

Roumestan, N. *Les supporters de football* (Paris: Anthropos, 1998).

Roversi, A. 'Calcio, Tifo, Violenza', *Rassegna Italiana di Sociologia* no. 4 (1986) 563–74.

Roversi, A. 'Calcio e violenza in Italia', in A. Roversi (ed.), *Calcio e violenza in Europa* (Bologna: Il Mulino, 1990) pp. 76–106.

Roversi, A. 'Football Violence in Italy', *International Review for the Sociology of Sport* 26(4) (1991) 311–32.

Roversi, A. 'The Birth of the "Ultras": the rise of football hooliganism in Italy', in R. Giulianotti and J. Williams (eds), *Game without Frontiers* (Aldershot: Arena, 1994) pp. 359–81.

Roversi, A. and Balestri, C. 'Italian Ultras Today: Change or decline?', *European Journal of Criminal Policy and Research* 8(2) (2000) 183–99.

Sack, A. and Suster, Z. 'Soccer and Croatian Nationalism', *Journal of Sport & Social Issues* 24(3) (2000) 305–20.

Sainati, G. and Bonelli, L. (eds) *La machine à punir* (Paris: L'Esprit frappeur, 2000/2004).

Salter, M. 'The Judges v. the Football Fan: a sporting contest?', *Northern Ireland Legal Quarterly* 36(4) (1985) 351–7.

Salter, M. 'Judicial Responses to Football Hooliganism', *Northern Ireland Legal Quarterly* 37(3) (1986) 280–93.

Salvini, A. (ed.) Il rito aggressivo (Florence: Giunti, 1988).

Scheppele, K. L. 'Law in a Time of Emergency: States of exception and the temptations of 9/11', *University of Pennsylvania Journal of Constitutional Law* 6 (2004) 1001–83.

Schlesinger, P. and Tumber, H. *Reporting Crime* (Oxford: Clarendon Press, 1994).

Schneider, H. J. 'Crime in the Mass Media', *Annales internationales de criminologie* 30, no. 1/2 (1992) 85–100.

Sellin, T. *Culture Conflict and Crime* (New York: Social Science Research Council, 1938).

Sénat (France) *Faut-il avoir peur des supporters?* Rapport no. 467 (26 September 2007).

Shaw, C. and McKay, H. *Juvenile Delinquency and Urban Areas* (Chicago: University of Chicago Press, 1969).

Shearing, C. 'Punishment and the Changing Face of the Governance', *Punishment & Society* 3(2), (2001) 203–20.

Sheptycki, J. 'Faire la police dans la Manche: l'évolution de la coopération transfrontalière (1968–1996)', *Cultures & Conflits* no. 26/27 (1997) 93–121.

Sheptycki, J. (ed.) *Issues in Transnational Policing* (London: Routledge, 2000).

Sheptycki, J. *In Search of Transnational Policing* (Aldershot: Ashgate, 2002).

Short, J. 'Gang Delinquency and Anomie', in M. B. Clinard (ed.), *Anomie and Deviant Behavior* (New York: The Free Press, 1964), pp. 98–127.

Silver, E. and Miller, L. 'A Cautionary Note on the Use of Actuarial Risk Assessment Tools for Social Control', *Crime & Delinquency* 48(1) (2002) 138–61.

Simon, G. 'Police des stades et libertés publiques: le dispositif préventif et répressif de lutte contre la violence en France et en Europe', in G. Simon (ed.), *Le stade et le droit* (Paris: Dalloz, 2008), pp. 179–90.

Simon, J. 'Governing through Crime', in L. M. Friedman and G. Fisher (eds) *The Crime Connection* (Boulder, CO: Westview Press, 1997), pp. 171–89.

Sims, P. N. and Tsitsoura, A. 'La Convention européenne sur la violence et les débordements des spectateurs lors des manifestations sportives et notamment les matches de football', *Revue de droit pénal et de criminologie* no. 5 (1987) 393–401.

Smolik, J. 'Football Hooliganism from the Standpoint of Extremism', *Central European Political Studies Review* VI (2004) <www.cepsr.com>.

Spaaij, R. *Understanding Football Hooliganism* (Amsterdam: Amsterdam University Press, 2006).

Spaaij, R. 'Football Hooliganism as a Transnational Phenomenon: Past and present analysis: a critique – more specificity and less generality', *The International Journal of the History of Sport* 24(4) (2007) 411–31.

Spector, M. and Kitsuse, J. I. *Constructing Social Problems* (Menlo Park, CA: Cummings, 1977).

Starmer, K. 'Setting the Record Straight: Human rights in an era of international terrorism', *European Human Rights Law Review* np. 2 (2007) 123–32.

Statewatch, *Public Order: Conflict management: Experts meeting in Brussels on 15 April 1998* (1998) <www.statewatch.org>.

Statewatch, *Public Order Policing in Europe – Policy Backlash Expected* (June 2001a) <www.statewatch.org>.

Statewatch, *The 'Enemy Within': EU Plans the Surveillance of Protestors and the Criminalisation of Protests* (November 2001b) <www.statewatch.org>.

Steinert, H. 'The Indispensable Metaphor of War: On populist politics and the contradictions of the state's monopoly of force', *Theoretical Criminology* 7 (2003) 265–91.

Stott, C. 'Police Expectations and the Control of English Soccer Fans at Euro 2000', *Policing: An International Journal of Police Strategies and Management* 26(4) (2003) 640–55.

Stott, C., Adang, O., Livingstone, A. et al. *Policing, Crowd Dynamics and Public Order at Euro 2004*, Final Report (London: Home Office, 2006).

Stott, C., Adang, O., Livingstone, A. et al. 'Variability in the Collective Behaviour of England Fans at Euro 2004: "Hooliganism", public order policing and social change', *European Journal of Social Psychology* 37(1) (2007) 75–100.

Stott, C. and Pearson, G. 'Football Banning Orders, Proportionality, and Public Order Policing', *The Howard Journal* 45(3) (2006) 241–54.

Stott, C. and Pearson, G. *Football 'Hooliganism'* (London: Pennant Books, 2007).

Stott, C. and Reicher, S. 'How Conflict Escalates: the inter-group dynamics of collective football crowd disorder', *Sociology* 32(2) (1998) 353–77.

Sutherland, E. and Cressey, D. *Principles of Criminology* (Philadelphia: Lippincott, 1960).

Suttles, G. *The Social Order of the Slum* (Chicago: The University of Chicago Press, 1968).

Szabo, D. *Criminologie* (Montréal: Les Presses de l'Université de Montréal, 1965).

Szabo, D. 'Le point de vue socio-culturel dans l'étiologie de la conduite délinquante', *Revue internationale des sciences sociales* 18(2) (1966) 193–211.

Tash, R. *Dutch Pluralism* (New York: Peter Lang, 1991).

Taylor, I. 'Hooligans: Soccer's Resistance Movement', *New Society* (7 August 1969) 204–6.

Taylor, I. 'Soccer Consciousness and Soccer Hooliganism', in S. Cohen (ed.), *Images of Deviance* (Harmondsworth: Penguin Books, 1971a), pp. 134–64.

Taylor, I. 'Football Mad: A Speculative Sociology of Football Hooliganism', in E. Dunning (ed.), *The Sociology of Sport* (London: Frank Cass, 1971b), pp. 352–77.

Taylor, I. 'Class, Violence and Sport', in H. Cantelon and R. Gruneau (eds), *Sport, Culture and the Modern State* (Toronto: University of Toronto Press, 1982a), pp. 39–96.

Taylor, I. 'On the Sports Violence Question: Soccer hooliganism revisited', in J. Hargreaves (ed.), *Sport, Culture and Ideology* (London: Routledge & Kegan Paul, 1982b), pp. 152–96.

Taylor, I. 'Il significato di Bruxelles', *Rassegna italiana di sociologia* no. 4 (1986) 598–601.

Taylor, I. and Wall, D. 'Beyond the Skinheads: Comments on the emergence and significance of the Glamrock cult', in G. Mungham and G. Pearson (eds), *Working Class Youth Culture* (London: Routledge & Kegan Paul, 1976), pp. 105–23.

Taylor, J. 'The War on Soccer Hooliganism: the European Convention on spectator violence and "misbehaviour" at sports events', *Virginia Journal of International Law* 27 (1987) 603–53.

Taylor, M. 'Football et culture politique en Grande-Bretagne', in Y. Gastaut and S. Mourlane (eds), *Le football dans nos sociétés* (Paris: Autrement, 2006), pp. 94–118.

Thompson, K. *Moral Panics* (London: Routledge, 1998).

Tilly, C. *La France conteste* (Paris: Fayard, 1986).

T.M.C. Asser Instituut, *Football Hooliganism with an EU Dimension* (The Hague: T.M.C. Asser Instituut, 2004).

Touraine, A. *La voix et le regard* (Paris: Seuil, 1978).

Treaty of Prüm on the Stepping-up of Cross–border Cooperation, Particularly in Combating Terrorism, Cross-border Crime and Illegal Migration (27 May 2005).

Trivizas, E. 'Offences and Offenders in Football Crowd Disorders', *The British Journal of Criminology* 20(3) (1980) 276–88.

Trivizas, E. 'Sentencing the "Football Hooligan" ', *The British Journal of Criminology* 21(4) (1981) 342–9.

Trivizas, E. 'Disturbances Associated with Football Matches', *The British Journal of Criminology* 24(4) (1984) 361–83.

Tsoukala, A. *Sport et violence* (Athens/Brussels: Sakkoulas/Bruylant, 1995).

Tsoukala, A. 'La gestion policière du hooliganisme: Angleterre, Italie, Pays-Bas', in J.-C. Basson (ed.), *Sport et ordre public* (Paris: IHESI/La Documentation française, 2001), pp. 159–174.

Tsoukala, A. 'Le traitement médiatique de la criminalité étrangère en Europe', *Déviance et société* 26(1) (2002) 61–82.

Tsoukala, A. 'Les nouvelles politiques de contrôle du hooliganisme en Europe: de la fusion sécuritaire au multipositionnement de la menace', *Cultures & Conflits* no. 51 (2003) 83–96.

Tsoukala, A. 'Democracy against Security: the debates about counter-terrorism in the European Parliament, September 2001–June 2003', *Alternatives* 29(4) (2004a) 417–39.

Tsoukala, A. 'La construction médiatique de la figure du hooligan dans la presse française', in Société de Sociologie du Sport de Langue Française, *Dispositions et pratiques sportives* (Paris: L'Harmattan, 2004b), pp. 345–60.

Tsoukala A., 'La lutte contre le crime organisé en Sicile. L'opération militaire Vespri Siciliani', *Cultures & Conflits* no. 56 (2004c) 51–61.

Tsoukala, A. 'Looking at Immigrants as Enemies', in D. Bigo and E. Guild (eds), *Controlling Frontiers* (Aldershot: Ashgate, 2005), pp. 161–92.

Tsoukala, A. 'Democracy in the Light of Security. British and French political discourses on domestic counterterrorism policies', *Political Studies* 54(3) (2006a) 607–27.

Tsoukala, A. 'Constructing the Threat in a Sports Context. British press discourses on football hooliganism', in J. Aquesolo (ed.), *Violence and Sport* (Seville: University Pablo de Olavide, 2006b), pp. 372–9.

Tsoukala, A. 'La légitimation des mesures d'exception dans la lutte antiterroriste en Europe', *Cultures & Conflits* no. 61 (2006c) 35–50.

Tsoukala A., 'The Security Issue at the 2004 Olympics', *European Journal for Sport and Society* 3(1) (2006d) 43–54.

Tsoukala, A. 'Defining Terrorism in the Post-September 11th Era', in D. Bigo and A. Tsoukala (eds), *Terror, Insecurity and Liberty* (London: Routledge, 2008a), pp. 49–99.

Tsoukala, A. 'Boundary-creating Processes and the Social Construction of Threat', *Alternatives* 33(2) (2008b) 139–54.

Tsoukala, A. 'Terrorist Threat, Freedom and Politics in Europe', in P. Noxolo and J. Huysmans (eds), *Security and Insecurity* (Basingstoke: Palgrave Macmillan, 2009).

Tsoukala, A., Basson, J.–C., Lestrelin, L. et al. *Les enjeux des dispositifs actuels de lutte contre le hooliganisme en France*, Final Report (Paris: Interior Ministry, 2008).

Tsouramanis, C. *I simperifora ton hooligans* (Athens: Sakkoulas, 1988).

Tulkens, F. 'La tragédie du Heysel: les responsabilités. Le débat sur le plan juridique', *Revue interdisciplinaire d'études juridiques*, special issue (1988) 71–141.

Tulkens, F. and Bosly, H. D. (eds) *La justice pénale et l'Europe* (Brussels: Bruylant, 1996).

UEFA, *Order and Security in the Stadia, Binding Instructions and Recommendations to Avoid Crowd Disturbances* (Nyon: UEFA, 1983).

UEFA, *Binding Safety and Security Instructions* (Nyon: UEFA, 2004).

Ungar, S. 'Moral Panic versus the Risk Society: the implications of the changing sites of social anxiety', *British Journal of Sociology* 52(2) (2001) 271–92.

Ünsal, A. 'Violences de stade en Turquie', in D. Yarsuvat and P.-H. Bolle (eds), *La violence et le fanatisme dans le sport* (Istanbul: University of Galatasaray, 2004), pp. 35–103.

Vakalopoulos, A. *Nea helliniki historia* (Thessalonica: Vanias, 1997).

Vassort, P. *Football et politique* (Paris: Passion, 1999).

Vaugrand, H. *Sociologies du sport* (Paris: L'Harmattan, 1999).

Vrcan, S. 'The Curious Drama of the President of a Republic versus a Football Tribe', *International Review for the Sociology of Sport* 1 (2002) 59–77.

Wacquant, L. *Les prisons de la misère* (Paris: Raisons d'agir, 1999a).

Wacquant, L. 'Des "ennemis commodes"', *Actes de la recherche en sciences sociales* no. 129 (1999b) 63–7.

Waddington, D. *Policing Public Disorder* (Cullompton: Willan Publishing, 2007).

Waddington, P. A. J. 'Dying in a Ditch: the use of police powers in public order', *International Journal of the Sociology of Law* 21(4) (1993) 335–53.

Waever, O. 'Securitization and Desecuritization', in R. Lipshutz (ed.), *On Security* (New York: Columbia University Press, 1995), pp. 46–86.

Waever, O., Buzan, B., Kelstrup, M. and Lemaitre, P. *Identity, Migration, and the New Security Agenda in Europe* (London: Pinter, 1993).

Wagg, S. *The Football World* (Brighton: Harvester Press, 1984).

Wahl, A. and Lafranchi, P. *Les footballeurs professionnels des années trente à nos jours* (Paris: Hachette, 1995).

Waldron, J. 'Security and Liberty: the image of balance', *The Journal of Political Philosophy* 11(2) (2003) 191–210.

Walgrave, L. and Limbergen, K. van 'Le hooliganisme belge: description et essai de compréhension', *Revue interdisciplinaire d'études juridiques*, special issue (1988) 7–31.

Walgrave, L. and Limbergen, K. van 'Il teppismo calcistico in Belgio: cause e rimedi', in A. Roversi (ed.), *Calcio e violenza in Europa* (Bologna: Il Mulino, 1990), pp. 139–67.

Ward, C. *Steaming in* (London: Simon & Schuster, 1989).

Warren, I. *Football, Crowd and Cultures*, ASSH Studies in Sports History, no. 13 (2003).

Webster, C. 'The construction of British "Asian" criminality', *International Journal of Sociology of the Law* 25(1) (1997) 65–86.

Webster, W. R. 'The Diffusion, Regulation and Governance of Closed-Circuit Television in the UK', *Surveillance & Society* 2(2/3) (2004) 230–50.

Weed, M. 'Ing-ger-land at Euro 2000', *International Review for the Sociology of Sport* 36(4) (2001) 407–24.

Weinreb, L. *Natural Law and Justice* (Cambridge, MA: Harvard University Press, 1987).

Weir, S. 'The Sewer Rats', *New Society* (14 August 1980) 319–20.

Weis, K. 'Tifosi di calcio nella Repubblica Federale Tedesca: violenze e provvedimenti', in A. Roversi (ed.) *Calcio e violenza in Europa* (Bologna: Il Mulino, 1990), pp. 55–78.

Welch, M., Price, E. and Yankey, N. 'Moral Panic over Youth Violence: Wilding and the manufacture of menace in the media', *Youth & Society* 34(1) (2002) 3–30.

Whannel, G. 'Football, Crowd Behaviour and the Press', *Media, Culture and Society* 1 (1979) 327–42.

Wieviorka, M. 'Le nouveau paradigme de la violence', *Cultures & Conflits* no. 29/30 (1998) 7–57.

Williams, J. 'Football Hooliganism: Offences, Arrests and Violence – a Critical Note', *British Journal of Law and Society* 7(1) (1980) 104–11.

Williams, J. 'The Brutes are Coming', *New Statesman and Society* (10 June 1988) 19.

Williams, J., Dunning, E. and Murphy, P. *Hooligans Abroad* (London: Routledge, 1984/1989).

Williams, J., Dunning, E. and Murphy, P. 'La strada verso l'Heysel', *Rassegna italiana di sociologia*, no. 4 (1986) 573–87.

Willis, P. *Common Culture* (Buckingham: Open University Press, 1990).

Wilson, J. Q. *Thinking about Crime* (New York: Basic Books, 1975).

Wilson, J. Q. and Kelling, G. L. 'Broken Windows: the police and neighborhood safety', *The Atlantic Monthly* (March 1982) <www.theatlantic.com>.

Wolfgang, M. E. and Ferracuti, F. *The Subculture of Violence* (London: Tavistock Publications, 1967).

Wolfgang, M. E., Figlio, R. M. and Sellin, T. *Delinquency in a Birth Cohort* (Chicago: University of Chicago Press, 1972).

Zahopoulos, C. *O politismos ton gipedon* (Thessalonica: Ianos, 2004).

Zani, B. and Kirchler, E. 'When Violence Overshadows the Spirit of Sporting Competition: Italian football fans and their clubs', *Journal of Community and Applied Social Psychology* 1(1) (1991) 5–21.

Name Index

Subject Index

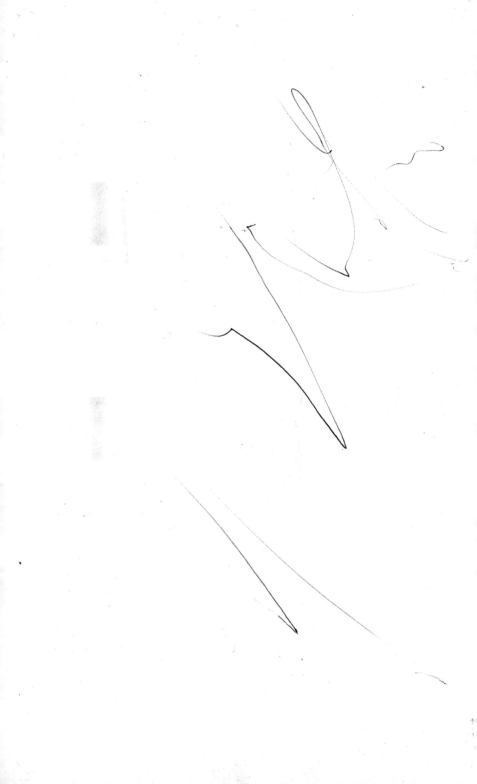